DIGITAL TECHNOLOGIES FOR GOVERNMENT-SUPPORTED HEALTH INSURANCE SYSTEMS IN ASIA AND THE PACIFIC

DECEMBER 2021

ADB

ASIAN DEVELOPMENT BANK

Some rights reserved. Published in 2021.

ISBN 978-92-9269-253-7 (print); 978-92-9269-254-4 (electronic); 978-92-9269-255-1 (ebook)
Publication Stock No. TCS210526
DOI: http://dx.doi.org/10.22617/TCS210526

The views expressed in this publication are those of the authors and do not necessarily reflect the views and policies of the Asian Development Bank (ADB) or its Board of Governors or the governments they represent.

ADB does not guarantee the accuracy of the data included in this publication and accepts no responsibility for any consequence of their use. The mention of specific companies or products of manufacturers does not imply that they are endorsed or recommended by ADB in preference to others of a similar nature that are not mentioned.

By making any designation of or reference to a particular territory or geographic area, or by using the term "country" in this document, ADB does not intend to make any judgments as to the legal or other status of any territory or area.

Please contact pubsmarketing@adb.org if you have questions or comments with respect to content, or if you wish to obtain copyright permission for your intended use that does not fall within these terms, or for permission to use the ADB logo.

Corrigenda to ADB publications may be found at http://www.adb.org/publications/corrigenda.

Note:
In this publication, "$" refers to United States dollars.
ADB recognizes "Korea" as the Republic of Korea and "Vietnam" as Viet Nam.

On the cover: Digital technologies are key to improve how health financing systems, including insurance schemes, can be more responsive to citizens, improving access to care, information retrieval, payments, and collaboration across actors in the system.

Cover design by Cleone Baradas.

Contents

Tables, Figures, and Boxes

Acknowledgments

Financed by the Republic of Korea e-Asia and Knowledge Partnership Fund, this report is based on analysis carried out in 2021 to inform governments and other stakeholders on how digital technology can be used to improve government-supported health insurance schemes across Asia and the Pacific. It is also intended to guide future program design and implementation initiatives of ADB particularly on digital health technology investments that support health financing mechanisms.

The report was prepared by ADB consultants Michael Stahl, Siddharth Srivastava, and Daniella Majakari, hired under contract with the Swiss Tropical Health Institute, along with inputs from and under the overall guidance of Arin Dutta, senior health specialist, and additional insights from Rui Liu, health specialist, from ADB's Sustainable Development and Climate Change Department (SDCC). It also benefitted from the review and inputs of Brian Chin, senior health specialist, from ADB's Central and West Asia Department.

Also acknowledged are the support of Michelle Apostol, associate health officer, and Sheela Myla O. Rances, operations analyst, from SDCC as well as the publishing team in ADB's Department of Communications.

Abbreviations

ADB	Asian Development Bank
AI	artificial intelligence
CRVS	Civil Registration and Vital Statistics System
EHR	electronic health record
EMR	electronic medical record
GS-NSPC	General Secretariat-National Social Protection Council
ICT	information and communication technology
IDs	identification systems
JLN	Joint Learning Network
LMIC	low- and middle-income country
NCD	noncommunicable disease
NHI	national health insurance
NHIIS	National Health Insurance Information System
NUIN	national universal unique identity numbers
PRC	People's Republic of China
SDCC	Sustainable Development and Climate Change Department
UHC	universal health coverage
UHI	Unique Health Identifier
USSD	Unstructured Supplementary Service Data
VSS	Vietnam Social Security

Executive Summary

Many countries in Asia and the Pacific continue to face challenges when it comes to health care and related services such as health insurance. Drawing on the experiences of selected countries, this report focuses on on the opportunities and good practices of how technologies can be used and integrated into government-supported health insurance schemes.

One of the noteworthy findings of this report is that there is no "best" or "most appropriate" solution for a particular country when selecting digital products to support the health insurer and that country contexts may vary widely. This is due in part to the complexity of public health financing and the e-health landscape of a particular country. Thus, the potential use and/or transferability of a particular digital solution need to be assessed on an individual basis.

The Asian Development Bank (ADB) requested a review to provide its developing member countries with an overview of how digital technology is being implemented and can support public health insurance operators in low- and middle-income countries (LMICs). This regional report on social health insurance technology was done through desk research alone using publicly available documentation as it was carried out at the height of the COVID-19 crisis.

The term "digital solution" in this report refers to all digital products and interventions that support a health insurance operator's business process and solutions that give the beneficiary better access to health insurance services. The authors have deliberately chosen this term because a digital solution is not necessarily a software product. It can also be a database or a mobile app, for instance. The authors do not reflect on the necessary baseline infrastructure that needs to be in place in a country to use digital products (electricity, internet) but is aware of different country contexts in this respect.

Another important distinction is between the use of phrases such as "national health insurance," "social health insurance schemes," and "public health insurance." In certain countries, these are not equivalent. The term "government-supported health insurance schemes" is used throughout this report as the focus is on schemes that are either implemented at the national level or where the government intends to do so in the medium and long terms. Therefore, where the terms "health insurer" and "health insurance scheme" are used in the following pages, it is assumed that government-supported health insurance schemes are meant.

The report aims to provide an overview of which digital solutions can support public health insurance operators' core business processes. Specific examples were given, mainly in LMICs when available, to show how these have been successfully implemented and used to improve operations. However, it was challenging to find these examples as it became apparent that there is very little publicly available documentation presenting the respective products and digital interventions for government-supported health insurance operators, especially in developing countries. Due to COVID-19 restrictions, on the ground research was not possible. Therefore, the authors reported examples from other contexts, such as developed countries or the private sector, to show best practices.

Software for health insurers is developed locally.

When looking at the country examples featured in this report, it is noticeable that the complexity of some digital solutions is sometimes slightly underestimated, especially when it comes to "upscaling" as soon as the number of beneficiaries and claims starts to increase.

Similarly, the complexity of digital solutions increases the more government stakeholders digitally interact with the health insurer. It is also evident that most software products that support public health insurers' business processes in Asian countries have been developed locally. The consultants believe that one reason for this is the lack of global, off-the-shelf software designed to meet health insurers' needs in developing countries. Moreover, the general complexity and dynamics of a specific health-care system make the development of "standard software" very difficult.

Collecting data alone does not help.

The analysis also showed the enormous potential of digital products and the power of data. Economies such as the Republic of Korea and Taipei,China with a very high digital maturity status today have already invested in digital health strategies about 10 years ago and have also built up a data-use culture among health system stakeholders. Moreover, these economies have created clear legal frameworks that regulate data exchange, data security, and data privacy, among other things.

Although, as mentioned previously, the primary focus of this report is not on private health insurance, it is worthy of mentioning that the research also showed that, while public health insurers are very interested in using digital products, the cutting-edge technical innovations come from private health insurers. This is not surprising as private insurers have a much greater interest in detailed datasets to evaluate insurance contracts individually, for underwriting purposes, and to make forecasts on potential health risks. On the other hand, most digital products on the public insurer side are used in the core business processes of member management, contribution collection, and claims management.

Many public health insurers are working on more advanced digital tools for member registration and management. Great hopes are being pinned on the use of artificial intelligence (AI) to revolutionize claims management. However, individual countries' success or failure depends very little on a specific technical solution itself.

Mobile payment options are the future.

Great added value is created when premium payment is linked to digital payment options via mobile phones so that the beneficiary no longer has to travel to a payment point. The key is to work with mobile payment service providers and telecom operators to keep transaction costs as low as possible.

Governments and development partners should take a cross-sectoral approach to promote alternative forms of payment. Instead of signing individual contracts with different mobile payment providers and promoting multiple technical gateways, investments in cross-government payment platforms should be considered. A cross-government payment hub can create benefits that go far beyond the needs of health insurance.

Demand for digitally supported claims management is high.

Many e-health and m-health but also e-government strategies indicate that digital support for more efficient claims management is high on the wish list of many national health insurers. The main reason for this is that it can bring significant time and cost savings for the insurer and the service provider and ultimately for the insured.

The advantage of regulated data exchange is crucial in claims management. Some countries are more advanced than others in defining these data standards and regulations for data exchange between the health service providers and the health insurers.

However, there is an increasing desire to use AI in claims management. On the subject of AI development, it is essential to know it requires much experience and a particular combination of skills to create algorithms that can teach machines to think, improve business processes, and optimize them. AI algorithms only work if the company has a clear idea of what is to be achieved and if the existing data quality is already high.

Digital health strategies can support smart digital investments.

Choosing the right digital tool requires interaction between the organizations and people involved in the health system—supported by good leadership from the government. In particular, a joint analysis of the practical benefits that a digital product can bring is of great importance.

It has been observed that countries with a clear vision, mission, and strategy for the long-term goals to be achieved in the health sector are also more successful in selecting appropriate digital products. If a potential digital solution does not contribute, respectively, to the strategic goals in the health sector and health financing, it may be a questionable investment.

Therefore, it is crucial to check whether the digital health strategy also considers the needs and requirements of health insurers so that a smooth interaction between service providers and insurers can be achieved with the help of digital connectivity.

Introduction and Methodology

In the public health domain, a critical development over the past 20 years involved the increase in the use of digital technologies for strengthening health systems as well as for the provision of social protection in low- and middle-income countries (LMICs). In line with this progress in the last 2 decades, the World Health Organization's *Global Strategy on Digital Health 2020–2025* also emphasizes the need for innovations that can lead to better information management, including improvements in digital health technologies that health workers can use to improve their efficiency.

Public health has become even more relevant given the current COVID-19 pandemic, which has generated additional demand for digital support. For instance, digital patient identification has become essential for effective contact tracing or vaccine distribution in the context of this pandemic. Another example is the increasing acceptance of telemedicine services, which avoid physical contact and thus virus spread.

Progressively, more countries are establishing Universal Health Coverage (UHC) as a goal around which national health financing strategies are designed or aligned. Countries are increasingly strengthening their health financing functions of revenue generation, pooling, and purchasing by creating or consolidating their respective forms of government-supported health insurance schemes. Technology is often a means to an end, and it is a crucial element of an efficient (cost-effective and sustainable) and successful National Health Insurance (NHI) that forms an integral part of these nations' health systems.

The use of intelligent information and communication technology (ICT) solutions to automate health insurance companies' business processes, reduce bureaucracy, and improve efficiency and transparency is urgently needed in many countries. However, public or semiautonomous health insurance agencies often lag far behind the private insurance industry, so they miss opportunities to enhance the experience for the insured.

The Asian Development Bank (ADB) is committed to building a prosperous, inclusive, resilient, and sustainable environment for Asia and the Pacific while putting significant efforts to eradicate poverty. The Operational Plan for Health 2015–2020 provides strategic directions for ADB's support to its developing members to strengthen health-care and health financing systems. Policies and programs outlined in this operational plan aim to help regions break the cycle of poverty, enhance growth through investment in human capital, increase productivity, and reduce people's vulnerability to risk.

At the same time, among the significant elements that comprise ADB's Social Protection Strategy, there are the government-supported health insurance schemes, which cushion the risks associated with unemployment, catastrophic out-of-pocket health costs, disability, work injury, and the growing ranks of the elderly. Strengthening NHI structures, including digitalization, is an essential priority for ADB, and it has invested in research and numerous resources such as the working paper on "Guidance for Investing in Digital Health."

In line with ADB's Operational Plan for Health, this report evaluates technologies used by national health insurers in Asia and the Pacific to disseminate knowledge about successful examples and to explore solutions for expanding them to scale. It aims to help countries in the region gain a clearer understanding of how digital tools may be used to manage the operations of their national health insurance organizations.

Mapping existing digital solutions for health financing operators can provide for country cases in LMICs that show how digital technologies can enhance health financing functions, impact other health financing blocks, and contribute to UHC progress.

This report is intended to show examples of innovative digital solutions that match the health insurance business processes of a government-supported health insurance scheme. The learning from these examples is also expected to show which basic technical infrastructure is required and the extent to which the health sector needs to engage with partners outside the health insurance domain. In particular, the report considers opportunities and good practices of integrating new technologies into government-supported health insurance schemes and will show successful examples of improvements in

(i) health insurance management and administration through digitization and innovative technologies, including provider payments and claims management and
(ii) services delivery through innovative technologies and partnerships.

The authors focused on existing literature such as gray literature, case studies, workshop presentations, and other freely available documentation showcasing solutions covering different business processes of health financing operators. The report preferably uses country examples from Asia and the Pacific but also the African continent. In some cases, the report points to examples from Europe, where significant learnings have been found. Additionally, a few examples from the private insurance sector are given to provide inspiration and ideas for government-supported health insurance systems.

This report is not meant to provide advice on the "best" or "most suitable" solution for a particular country as country contexts differ, and the potential transferability of particular digital solutions should be assessed on an individual basis. Instead, the authors hope that collecting available digital solutions will provide innovative ideas and approaches that contribute to a technical dialogue among health system stakeholders (especially NHIs) in LMICs and facilitate decision-making for the use of digital interventions.

Digital Health Ecosystem for Health Insurance Operators

I

Digital technology has changed the quality of our lives in a remarkably flexible way concerning income levels. Although there are still significant disparities globally between rich and poor, there seems to be a homogeneity regarding the spread of mobile and internet connectivity across the world. Whether in Bhutan, Europe, India, the United Kingdom, the United States, or Viet Nam, most people in either country can catch up on vital health-care trends or locate the nearest health clinic online via their mobiles or increasingly pay for services, as an example, via their mobile phones.

For clarity and consistency, the authors provide definitions of key terminologies used in this report, which also lays out the scope of this report.

Digital Health Technology. There are several definitions available for digital health technology. This report refers to all digital products and interventions that support the business process of a health insurance operator and solutions that give the beneficiary better access to health insurance services.

National Health Insurance Information System (NHIIS). This term is defined by the Joint Learning Network (JLN) for Universal Health Coverage, a network of practitioners and policymakers collaborating to address challenges and produce solutions to implementing reforms toward universal health coverage.[1] NHIIS is defined as an ICT solution implemented to support operations and management of national health insurance schemes. There are three main actors in health insurance schemes: the beneficiary, payer, and provider. At the very minimum, the goal of the ICT solution as an NHIIS should be to accommodate the processes and interactions that take place among the three actors, as shown in Figure 1.

Universal Health Coverage. One fundamental assumption of this report is that digital technologies for health financing, including health insurance, should promote UHC connected with the United Nations Sustainable Development Goal No. 3 on Health.[2] UHC is defined in line with the WHO definition as ensuring that all people have access to needed quality health services and that the use of these services does not expose users to financial hardship. Financial protection is a vital part of attaining UHC, but even the best digital intervention is useless if the potential beneficiary cannot benefit from this solution or that the cost and/or time-saving aspects are marginal.

---

[1] Joint Learning Network for Universal Health Coverage. 2019. *A Guide to Common Requirements for National Health Insurance Information Systems.* PATH.

[2] United Nations. 2021. *Goal 3: Ensure Healthy Lives and Promote Well-Being for All at All Ages.* [online] Available from: https://www.un.org/sustainabledevelopment/health/ (accessed 20 May 2021).

Figure 1: Interactions among Actors of Health Insurance Schemes

Payer

Beneficiary

Provider

1. Enroll

2. Pay Premium*

7. Submit Claims

6. Contracting
8. Process Claims

3. Pay Co-payment*

4. Membership Verification
5. Provide Care

*if required

Source: Authors.

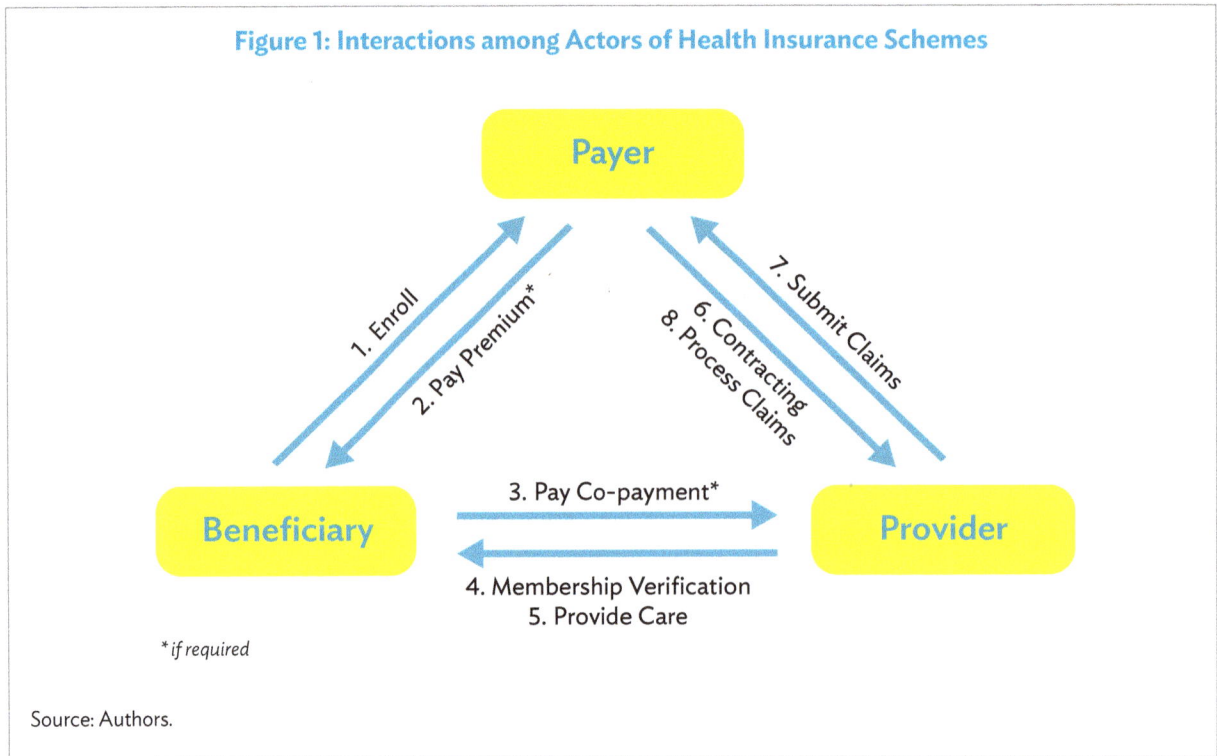

Hence, various digital tools in the health sector have interactions, overlaps, and linkages with NHIIS systems in any country, where national insurers are increasing part of government plans to move progressively toward UHC. The examples of solutions discussed in this report fall within this subset of the digital health ecosystem.

The National Health Insurance Framework

A vast amount of literature suggests that a modern service organization requires scalable IT infrastructure.[3] Such scalable IT infrastructure is also applicable to the health sector, and thus, health insurance companies should be investing in digital solutions, ideally in a uniform company-wide system, and begin the transition into a modern service provider.

For a health insurance operator, it is vital that a digital solution specifically maps the business process of that organization and serves the employees as a tool for their daily work for it to be sustainable. To support mapping the business processes, the JLN initiative has drafted a structured framework (Figure 2) to organize the business processes of an insurer and to illustrate the significant functional areas and related business processes. The authors use this as a framework to structure this report, looking at successful examples from various developing countries that support such business processes.

The JLN framework is relevant for government-supported health insurance schemes as it was originally developed based on insights shared by practitioners in the public health-care systems of member counties, including national health insurers. Hence, the processes cover a range of transactions between insurers and beneficiaries where contributions are collected, as well with service providers to whom payments are made (physicians and hospitals) through different provider payment mechanisms (e.g., capitation, fee for service, Diagnosis-Related Groups). The JLN framework does not include the processes of private insurance companies where, for example, other business processes such as underwriting and personal risk assessment are involved.

This framework enables countries to understand the diversity of business processes and to look at their dependencies to each other. Additionally, by defining the major process groups, this framework creates flexibility for a range of health insurance scheme designs. While, for instance, some schemes may not require beneficiary enrollment and others may, both system types will require some level of beneficiary management.

---

3   Labrique, A. B. et al. 2018. Best Practices in Scaling Digital Health in Low and Middle-Income Countries. *Globalization and Health*, 14 (103).

Figure 2: Structured View of a National Health Insurance Framework, Organizing Business Processes by Functional Area

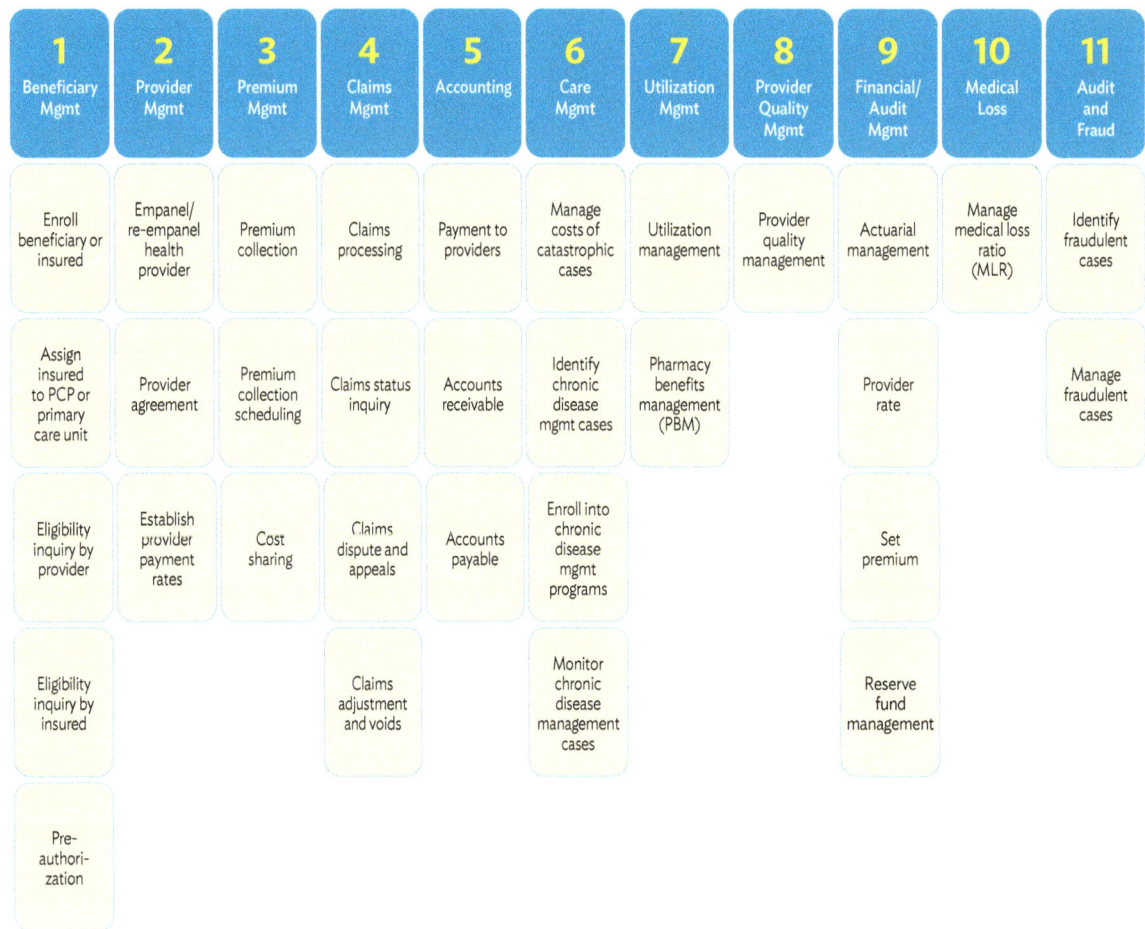

1 Beneficiary Mgmt	2 Provider Mgmt	3 Premium Mgmt	4 Claims Mgmt	5 Accounting	6 Care Mgmt	7 Utilization Mgmt	8 Provider Quality Mgmt	9 Financial/ Audit Mgmt	10 Medical Loss	11 Audit and Fraud
Enroll beneficiary or insured	Empanel/ re-empanel health provider	Premium collection	Claims processing	Payment to providers	Manage costs of catastrophic cases	Utilization management	Provider quality management	Actuarial management	Manage medical loss ratio (MLR)	Identify fraudulent cases
Assign insured to PCP or primary care unit	Provider agreement	Premium collection scheduling	Claims status inquiry	Accounts receivable	Identify chronic disease mgmt cases	Pharmacy benefits management (PBM)		Provider rate		Manage fraudulent cases
Eligibility inquiry by provider	Establish provider payment rates	Cost sharing	Claims dispute and appeals	Accounts payable	Enroll into chronic disease mgmt programs			Set premium		
Eligibility inquiry by insured			Claims adjustment and voids		Monitor chronic disease management cases			Reserve fund management		
Pre-authori-zation										

Source: Joint Learning Network for Universal Health Coverage. 2019. *A Guide to Common Requirements for National Health Insurance Information Systems.* PATH.

III Enabling Implementation

This chapter considers and describes two critical enablers for introducing digital solutions: digital health strategies and the correct assessment of the political landscape. It also provides insights on the innovations by private insurers and potential lessons for government-supported health insurers.

Digital Strategies and Their Relevance for Health Insurers

Many developing countries look into Europe, the Republic of Korea, or Japan to learn from their experience in formulating a strategy to use technology as an opportunity for expanding their existing health insurance schemes. While it is useful to look beyond borders to see what has worked well in more developed countries and where their challenges lie, the context needs to be taken into consideration as well.

It is important to stress that any innovative technological solution needs to be continuously assessed to ensure that the outcomes of introducing the solution continue to contribute to the long-term goals stated in the national digital health strategy.

It is observed that countries that have a clear vision, mission, and strategy for the goals to be achieved in the health sector are also faster in defining digital strategies. A clear goal, defined in a digital strategy, is the basis for assessing the reliability, sustainability, and cost-effectiveness of a potential digital intervention for a health insurance operator.

Especially in the health insurance arena, there is a tendency to compare country contexts incorrectly. An example of this would be smaller European countries such as Finland, Denmark, and Sweden. These are far ahead in using digital technologies for their citizens, but not only in the health sector.

However, this is due to specific factors such as:

- The countries are relatively "rich," and the government can afford a large portion of the budget for investments in digital health and/or on e-governance interventions.
- The government is centralized, and ministerial representatives are working closely together.
- The government formulated precise roadmaps and defined medium- and long-term goals before discussing potential digital solutions.
- The government invested in infrastructure development and IT literacy of the entire population.
- The government put effort into setting up "registries" and assigning a National Identifier to each citizen, which helps link to various programs and their digital tools.

The aforementioned characteristics are not present in many LMICs. An important difference is the comparatively high number of inhabitants, and thus, the number of potential health insurance beneficiaries differs significantly.

It is sensible to work on a digital health strategy that takes the health insurance side into account. However, "copying" digital health strategies from other country contexts does not work in practice.

While the need for better connected digital solutions for health insurance operators has already been recognized, it has also been recognized that this cannot work without a clear digital strategy that considers the country context and includes aspects outside the health sector (e.g., identification and biometrics[4]).

In the Lao People's Democratic Republic and Cambodia, where consolidation, merging, or linkages of existing health insurance schemes are currently under discussion, these countries have decided to develop their country-specific strategies that consider lessons learned from other countries. In Box 1, the ideal case of Estonia is presented, where a high level of digital maturity has been reached thanks to clear digital strategies.

BOX 1

Digital Strategies in Estonia

A good example that shows how these factors contributed to the successful implementations of digital health strategies is Estonia. Indeed, Estonia took its first steps toward e-health in 2004. In 2005, the government adopted the first e-health roadmap, and in 2008, the national health information system was launched. Since then, several additional services have been introduced. For example, e-prescribing began in 2010, and in 2018, all prescriptions were digital. E-consultations, which allow family doctors to consult virtually with specialists, were introduced in 2012. In 2015, their ambulances went digital, and in 2016, they introduced decision support systems to notify doctors about drug interactions. In 2018, the government continued its work by focusing on personalized medicine, enhanced analytics and research, and cross-border services.

Introducing e-health in Estonia was mainly based on good governance, committed stakeholders, a clear policy and strategy, and clear benefit(s) for its citizens. The relatively small size of the country, with a population of 1.3 million, was undoubtedly an advantage for technical implementers.

Source: Metsallik, J. et al. 2019. *Ten Years of the e-Health System in Estonia*. Department of Health Technologies, Tallinn University of Technology.

---

4   ADB. 2016. *Identity for Development in Asia and the Pacific*. Manila.

BOX 2

Takeaways for Digital Strategies

- The complexity of the insurance landscape has generally increased.
- Government-supported health insurers in Asia have very different levels of maturity in terms of digitalization. Some are still at the early stages of digital development, and there are not yet many examples of fully mature health insurers that are, for example, fully interconnected with health-care providers.
- The formulation of a digital health strategy can help governments stay on track and introduce digital solutions in a coherent manner.
- Digital strategy needs to be updated regularly.
- Ideally, the digital health strategy should contribute to the objectives of the overall health strategy of the country.
- There is a risk that too many different strategies with narrow focus are developed and not linked: it needs to be examined whether a digital strategy only for health insurance makes sense (if there are no existing broader ICT strategies) or if it should be integrated into another (especially when there is a broader framework).

Source: Authors.

The Importance of Politics

The design and implementation of a national health insurance scheme and digital support through adequate tools are a technical process and a political one. Indeed, stakeholders' views and support will determine how a country will implement digital solutions to ensure overall feasibility for health insurers. The introduction of digital tools on a national scale in developing countries often goes beyond operational needs and involves several ministries, health providers, consumers, employers, and donors.

Cambodia is a good example of a highly fragmented political and development partner landscape that has become more consolidated in recent years.

The key to greater transparency among all stakeholders was establishing the General Secretariat-National Social Protection Council (GS-NSPC). Its main task is to coordinate an integrated digital social (health) protection system as an umbrella organization.

This involves regular meetings with all political stakeholders, health system operators such as hospitals and health insurance funds, and related ministries to work on a nationwide digital platform that will allow better service provision.

Policymakers wanting to introduce a digital health strategy and solutions need to understand and be able to articulate the following to position their plans favorably:

- ◗ How does health insurance currently contribute to overall national health goals?
- ◗ Is there already a digital strategy available for the health sector?
- ◗ Who are the main actors, and what are their positions on development or expansion?
- ◗ What are possible policy barriers to the introduction of digital solutions?
- ◗ What are possible mitigation strategies?
- ◗ How can a political coalition be built to push for health insurance reforms and ensure they involve digital solutions?

In certain countries, there exists a common misunderstanding that the government ICT department takes full responsibility for the digitalization process. This misunderstanding is only partly true as a government ICT department, while critical, is not necessarily the strategic driver for digital change. Therefore, it is essential to note that digital health care is not only about the actual technology but also the broader social ambition of finding new ways of solving health-care problems, creating unique experiences for patients, accelerating health-care providers' growth, and delivering health-care services at an affordable price. From an NHI perspective, the cross-sectoral progress on the digitalization front is also an essential driver of change, e.g., robust digital approaches and ICT solutions for civil registration systems driven by the social welfare sector e-governance initiatives, which consequently contribute to the pace of technological innovations for NHI.

This issue is an important aspect, which has become apparent in various country analyses: The decision-maker's ability to separate the most technically innovative solutions from the most practical ones. Of course, the best-case scenario would be to find a solution that embodies both these characteristics—but unfortunately, this is a rare outcome.

Politicians often promote more charismatic technology that looks good rather than thinking about practicality and what is needed. A fictitious example would be a high investment in a modern smart card that only a few national hospitals can use to claim the respective customer's claim processing instead of a low-cost development of a mobile app that allows the insured to find and seek care at the nearest health-care provider.

A solution that only saves a marginal amount of time or money for key stakeholders will not survive in the long run, despite how nice it looks or how well it is advertised during the product launch.

BOX 3

Takeaways for the Importance of Politics

- Decision-makers should separate the most technically innovative solutions from the most practical ones.
- Government ICT departments should be involved in decision-making on digital solutions but should not necessarily be the strategic driver.
- Cross-sectoral approaches help governments discover digital solutions that can be used by as many government stakeholders as possible, apart from building buy-in this helps make the cost–benefit ratio very attractive.

Source: Authors.

The Role of Private Insurers

Compared with public insurers, private insurers are also concerned about how risk is pooled, but they deal with underwriting, claims management, and risk assessment at times from a different perspective, especially when profit-oriented. These operations have not changed radically within the past few years, but their effectiveness and efficiency have improved dramatically using digital technology.

Recent reports, such as the Health Insurance Top Trends 2021 report,[5] point out the benefits of well-aligned digital products for private insurers and how business process optimizations help the private insurance industry extend its coverage and win new clients.

Globally, private insurers are engaging with so-called InsurTechs in a variety of ways. This term makes use of technology innovations to increase savings and efficiency from the current insurance industry model. The term is a combination of the words "insurance" and "technology," inspired by the creation of the term FinTech. This recognition has led to the setting up of internal innovation centers or incubation cells and collaborations with InsurTechs, which have established offerings for specific applications or are investing in start-ups at various stages of development.

An interesting example of the inclusion of healthy lifestyle aspects in health insurance premiums comes from the private insurer Vitaly.[6] The UK-based company offers bonus points for a healthy lifestyle, which then contribute to lower premiums for the insured.

A particular invaluable asset that this collaboration with InsurTechs brings is within the field of data analytics. Indeed, the private industry has an advantage over several other industries concerning the potential availability of data. Many insurers have started using the opportunities offered by modern data analytics. Early movers in big data analytics, such as Viet Nam,[7] can offer better services to their customers and consequently get ahead of their competitors. Over the next few years, the need to leverage analytics will only increase and become a must to stand out over the competition.

Overall, it is essential to note that public insurers in the region can learn from their private counterparts and foster an environment conducive to innovation, especially for data analytics, and explore how their methods can be used in the context of a public health insurance scheme.

---

5   Capgemini. 2020. *Health Insurance Top Trends 2021*. Capgemini.
6   Vitality. 2021. *How We Work Out Your Health Insurance Renewal Premium*. [online] Vitality. Available from: https://www.vitality.co.uk/ health-insurance/renewal-rates/ (accessed 16 April).
7   Bui et al. 2021. Big Data for Public Health Surveillance in Vietnam: Challenges and Opportunities. *In: Kreinovich V. and Hoang Phuong N., eds. Soft Computing for Biomedical Applications and Related*. Springer International Publishing.

BOX 4

Takeaways for the Role of Private Insurers

- The higher share of innovations in the digital health insurance space generally comes from the private sector rather than the public one.
- The private sector has an advantage in terms of availability of data, on which they capitalize to improve their processes.
- Public health insurers can learn from private insurers in terms of digitization as they have already invested in building digital solutions a decade ago.

Source: Authors.

IV Health Insurance Business Processes

This chapter examines the core business processes of government-supported health insurance with the view of presenting future digitalization possibilities for LMICs.

The core processes of the JLN framework,[8] as described in previous chapters, were used. However, additional literature on social protection and e-government was also used, as it often provides hints on how to improve the interoperability of existing legacy software for health insurers.

The business process has been divided into three sections: First, a general background on the process and what it does. Second, key drivers, which can be seen as a set of critical factors for health insurers that provide a possible motivation for the use of digital technology. For example, a key driver can be a specific operational problem and a desire to save costs or improve customer service. Third, a few examples are presented to illustrate good practice. The focus for these examples is on LMIC contexts, but the authors also believe it is relevant to draw on experience from other contexts.

Beneficiary Management

Digital interventions can contribute to UHC in a variety of ways. For instance, they can remove financial as well as administrative barriers to access adequate and affordable health care.

There are three main barriers to the expansion of health insurance coverage:[9]
1. **The inability to enroll in schemes**. Complex or unclear communication on eligibility criteria creates potential challenges in enrollment, and complicated administrative mechanisms result in the exclusion of target groups.
2. **The inability to use the system**. After they have enrolled, participants in a health insurance scheme sometimes do not have access to the legally entitled benefit—and which may reveal the administrative inability of the public sector scheme to provide benefits for all those entitled to them.
3. **Inability to receive appropriate and high-quality services**. Members who succeed in overcoming obstacles to enroll may still not receive adequate protection. Health insurance coverage must be appropriate to the needs of each person, especially those from high-risk groups such as children, women, the elderly, or households exposed to other forms of discrimination.

---

8   Joint Learning Network for Universal Health Coverage. 2019. *A Guide to Common Requirements for National Health Insurance Information Systems*. PATH.

9   Odeyemi, I. A. 2014. *Community-Based Health Insurance Programmes and the National Health Insurance Scheme of Nigeria: Challenges to Uptake and Integration. International Journal for Equity in Health*. 13 (20).

In the case of health insurers, the admission of members and the verification of eligibility are categorized as beneficiary management.

Good digital beneficiary management in the insurance industry brings improvements in revenues, cost efficiency, and customer satisfaction. However, despite existing technology, the customer approach is still far from being consistently digitized and value-oriented in some cases.

Several technologies can aid the process of beneficiary management in developing countries. For example, an online eligibility check has extra advantages in countries with a high proportion of domestic migration or areas with many seasonal workers not covered via a formal health insurance scheme that runs for a whole year. Particularly when it comes to scheme portability, coverage gaps or double insurance issues should be avoided as much as possible, which online and real-time eligibility checks can help with. Decentralized information (e.g., on smart cards) that can be retrieved on the sport can as well aid beneficiary management processes in developing countries, though challenges with synchronization of decentralized data and cost of associated hardware are at times as well considerable. With improving internet connectivity, including in rural areas, the trade-off between centralized online retrieval and/or verification of data should be weighed against decentralized data storage options.

Very often, member database "silos" exist. A silo means that different health insurance operators each maintain their member databases without being linked. As a result, seamless tracking of a person throughout the entire health insurance landscape is impossible due to the lack of a uniform database or ID numbers.

Table 1: Key Drivers for Beneficiary Management

Challenge/Key driver	Digital support opportunities
Health insurers want to identify their beneficiaries	Ideally, the beneficiary database should be interoperable with other relevant national databases (e.g., CRVS system; Social Registry; National ID database)
Timely enrollment of beneficiaries and ease of use	Mobile enrollment apps Employee registration platform
Fraud and abuse should be prevented	Use of biometrics Online eligibility check
Redundant entries in the beneficiary database should be avoided	Use of biometrics

Source: Authors.

Addressing the Key Drivers and Solutions from Other Countries

This section takes a closer look at the areas of beneficiary identification, mobile enrollment apps, and portability of services.

Identification

At the basis of any government-supported health insurance schemes lies the challenge of person/citizen deification and the related role of Identification Numbers (IDs). Indeed, unique identification is a way of verifying or authenticating each person and aggregates data personally.

Gelb, A. & Clark, J. (2013)[10] state that some countries provide a general identification mechanism for their entire population using foundational ID systems. These mechanisms may include a Civil Registration Database as well as a unique national ID. Other countries opt for functional ID systems for a particular service, such as health-care provisioning. Indeed, a 2014 Survey by the World Bank's ID4D Working Group[11] provided evidence that, out of 198 countries, a majority still employ fragmented, single-purpose ID systems. This ID4D group Survey, together with several other reports, highlighted that it would be costly to introduce national identification mechanisms and that time would be needed to remove duplicates. Therefore, several authors recognized that the introduction, or upgrading, of identification mechanisms requires appropriate management structures and clear goals to enable interoperability among all health system operators.

The significance of identification systems and IDs has created a strong interest among many governments, particularly in developing countries, to understand better the advantages and disadvantages of linking existing IDs or creating a national ID covering full citizenship. Many studies note that different ID systems have been developed for different purposes:

- A central identification system and one of the oldest is the Civil Registration and Vital Statistics System (CRVS), which records birth, death, marriage, divorce, adoption, and issues identification documents such as birth certificates.
- Functional IDs are ID cards, numbers, or other systems created for specific government services, such as in the health sector, a health insurance card (Gelb and Clark, 2013).
- Foundational IDs are not linked to specific services but serve as legal proof of identity for multipurposes, such as a National ID Card that can access health services and other sectors such as banking (Gelb and Clark, 2013).

Foundational IDs are essential for health insurance and other benefit programs within the health system, given the fact that to access health facilities and therapies, a person in a particular country must prove that they are insured and what their entitlement is against what they contribute.

Additionally, IDs are essential elements for tracking valid payments to health facilities. Failure to provide proper documentation can result in the denial of benefits. Similarly, insurers and health-care providers may find more fraud cases if there is a lack of identification of beneficiaries. In some cases where health information systems are fragmented, patients may be billed twice, providers may be paid twice, or patients may not be adequately reimbursed when they seek treatment at multiple facilities.

Review of literature also shows that the form of ID systems in the health sector has also been evolving—paper-based ID systems, for example, are now primarily digital.[12] However, this does not mean that the number of IDs has decreased. Digital tools provide the opportunity to store data centrally and thus limit the need for multiple data collection; however, since a beneficiary database can be installed so quickly nowadays, many identifiers are being generated in parallel.

10   Gelb, A. and Clark, J. 2013. *Identification for Development: The Biometrics Revolution*. Centre for Global Development.
11   ID4D. 2021. *ID4D Data: Global Identification Challenge by the Numbers*. [online] The World Bank Group. Available from: https://id4d.worldbank.org/global-dataset (accessed 16 April).
12   Mills, S. et al. 2019. Unique Health Identifiers for Universal Health Coverage. *Journal of Health, Population and Nutrition*. 38 (22).

With more countries moving toward digital health solutions, patients identification options are expanding at the point of care and include:

- ⊙ using national universal unique identity numbers (NUINs) and also use these as National Unique Health Identifier (UHI),
- ⊙ developing and implementing an ID number mapping system based on an existing UHI, and
- ⊙ developing UHIs independently of the development of national IDs and CRVS systems and linking them.

Ultimately, insurance systems require complete and accurate health-care service utilization to bill patients, pay providers, and sustainably make budgeting and business decisions. The integration of unique identification mechanisms (e.g., a unique health ID) into health insurance programs improves effectiveness and efficiency in increasing coverage.

It is expected that the use of a unique national ID for the proper administration of health protection will bring several benefits such as:

- ⊙ reducing operational costs for beneficiary management, as those who wish to participate in a scheme, will not be excluded,
- ⊙ enabling the registration of beneficiaries when they move within the country,
- ⊙ eliminating duplicate or incorrect beneficiary entries and hence reducing fraud,
- ⊙ facilitating electronic payments through the banking sector, and
- ⊙ cross-referencing from one program to another to improve program integration and impact for beneficiaries.

Two successful implementations of nationwide ID systems are presented in Boxes 5 and 6.

BOX 5

National Identification Systems in the Republic of Korea

A country that successfully established a robust CRVS system, which benefited the National Insurance Fund and other government institutions, is the Republic of Korea. Indeed, the government has a very structured approach and assigns the Resident Registration (RR) numbers immediately at birth. Initially, no biometric features are recorded, but the child records are linked with the legal guardian's data. Then, at 17 years old, a fingerprint scan is also required, and a card is issued.

This lifelong identification number acts as the "golden key" for networking all digital solutions in the health-care system and beyond. Due to this precise identification and authorization process, the National Health Insurance Fund can efficiently complete specific tasks such as sending notification letters of free health checks to beneficiaries and drawing attention to a wide range of services.

Source: Kang, M. et al. 2019. *Korean Resident Registration System for Universal Health Coverage*. World Bank Group.

BOX 6

National Identification Systems in Thailand

This approach has been similarly implemented in Thailand. When a baby is born, either the hospital or the village headman issues a registration form to the child's parents. The parents bring the form together with their proof of identity to register the child's birth. At the district registrar's office, the registrar can check the information submitted against the information in the central database to register the child, issue a birth certificate, and assign the child a Personal Identification Number (PID). From this point on, the PID will be used to determine if the child is a Thai citizen, and if so, the child will be automatically enrolled in the National Health Insurance Scheme.

Since Thai citizens with a PID receive free health care and government child allowance, this incentive has increased the demand for birth registration. As in the Republic of Korea, this identification number is used for the health insurance system and multiple social services, and although the health information system at each hospital creates its patient identification numbers, these are linked to the patient's national PIDs. Health workers then use the PIDs to check patient eligibility, track health services, and process claims, among other activities.

Source: Mills, S. et al. 2019. Unique Health Identifiers for Universal Health Coverage. *Journal of Health, Population and Nutrition.* 38 (22).

Mobile enrollment apps

Mobile enrollment solutions can be divided into three categories:
1. solutions for self-enrollment that allows a potential beneficiary to enroll himself/herself in the health insurance scheme,
2. solutions where a third party does the enrollment—which could be an employer or an "agent" who takes care of specific population groups' enrollments, and
3. solutions where health insurance employees take over the registration (e.g., through mobile enrollment units).

Three examples are given to illustrate the three categories of enrollment solutions: in Indonesia, Kenya, and Nepal.

BOX 7

Mobile Enrollment App in Indonesia

One example of an app covering the first category (solutions for self-enrollment) is the mobile app, Mobile JKN, used in the Indonesian National Health Insurance program (BPJS Kesehatan). Various features that beneficiaries can use include the registration to the scheme view billing information, select or change primary health-care provider, set appointments, status checks, and file complaints. According to an ILO report on the digital solution, it has significantly helped extend the coverage of the health insurance scheme. A key success factor has been the collaboration with local governments and service providers to improve the outreach and usability of the app. Indonesia is an archipelago with more than 13,000 islands, which can make it difficult for people outside of urban areas to access services.

Handayani, et al. (2018) examined the critical success factors (CSFs) to guarantee the successful implementation and development of the Mobile JKN application. Success factors are arranged in order of highest to lowest weight:
- easy access;
- sufficient and relevant information;
- ease of user service;
- accuracy of information; and
- ease of reading.

However, other work could map the CSFs within the demographic variables to understand the factors that might influence certain groups of people. Handayani also concluded that a good mobile app should also serve to shorten the queue in hospitals but also reduce referral times.

Source: Handayani, P. W. 2018. Critical Success Factors for Mobile Health Implementation in Indonesia. *Heliyon*. 4 (11).

BOX 8

Mobile Enrollment App in Kenya

Another good example that shows enrollment types 1 and 2 comes from Kenya called M-TIBA, which CarePay developed. Insurers and health-care providers use it for the secure digital administration of large-scale health schemes via mobile phones. It allows members to manage their medical insurance benefits using their mobile phones while also providing real-time data exchange between patients, insurers, and health-care providers.

Agents and beneficiaries doing the registration are required to take a survey. The beneficiary then receives an activation text and is directed to dial a number to accept the terms and conditions. It has also contributed to the fight against COVID-19 by assisting the health-care sector in the deployment of mobile technology. Other recent developments include using contactless systems to verify patients seeking treatments at hospitals.

Source: NHIF. 2021. *NHIF Service Charter*. [online] NHIF Kenya. Available from: http://www.nhif.or.ke/healthinsurance/serviceCharter (accessed 2 February).

BOX 9

Mobile Enrollment App in Nepal

An example that embodies the third enrollment type can be found in Nepal. In the Nepal Social Health Insurance Scheme (Health Insurance Board), households are actively approached by an enrollment assistant to inform them about SHI availability. The enrollment assistant then registers the household via a mobile enrollment app. A more detailed description of the Nepali case will be presented further below in the report. One version of the mobile app is used to capture the picture of all individuals who are enrolled directly. Another version of the same mobile app was implemented in Tanzania, which takes the registration by an enrollment officer beyond just the picture. In this case, the app is also used to capture all details of the individual and payment collection information, thereby making the enrollment process fully digital, and in case full payment is made using mobile money, or in cash, the activation of the policy can happen on the spot.

Source: OpenIMIS. 2021. *Nepal.* [online] Schweizerische Eidgenossenschaft, Federal Ministry for Economic Cooperation and Development, Deutsche Gesellschaft für Internationale Zusammenarbeit. Available from: http://openimis.org/nepal (accessed 2 February).

Portability of services and eligibility check

Tracking an individual's insurance status throughout their life can be a challenge, especially in countries that do not have single universal insurance. Ideally, a health-care provider should know where a patient is insured in real time and, if not, who will finance their treatment, and which can be addressed through a well-designed Identification System and related ID number.

The unique identification of a beneficiary is related to the portability of insurance services. For a beneficiary, portability either relates to the design of a benefits package, the insured's geographical locations, or both. To achieve complete portability of benefits, a citizen in region A should travel to region B and receive the same level of medical treatment covered by their insurance if needed.

However, portability is also worth considering when someone changes the insurance operator (only relevant for some countries where people choose different insurance providers). An example of this is sickness benefits, where the duration of payment is based on the length of membership with a particular health insurer.

To attain this, it is necessary to differentiate whether a government health insurance scheme:
- offers a uniform and countrywide benefit package,
- presents regional (e.g., district-level) differences, or
- ties beneficiaries to a specific set of facilities.

Additionally, the service package might differ according to insurance product or target group (e.g., formal versus informal sector, poor households, migrants, and others), which has to be taken into account when designing portability options. Even though the primary benefits are regulated by law in many countries, some statutory health insurance funds can offer a wide range of additional benefits and services. An example country for this is Germany, where additional services, such as natural healing methods or improved dental care services, are provided by some statutory health insurance funds but not by all. Often a mix of situations is present in developing and transitional countries.

In highly populated countries such as Bangladesh, India, and Pakistan, the portability of social health insurance benefits for seasonal workers between administrative territories (especially between states) is a significant concern.[13] An extreme form of nonportability can arise when migrants leave their existing health insurance system and are unable or are denied access to a new system in their new state or district. In less extreme forms, migrants may no longer be able to use their earlier scheme to get admission to a full range of health services, or they may not be offered comparable coverage at a comparable cost under a new scheme (maybe because they are unable to pay net premiums which were made in their former system). Members who leave one state's health insurance system because they move to another state should not suffer any financial loss or unexpected gains due to mobility at the same time.

From a technological perspective, there is no golden rule for ensuring portability within the SHI sector. One type of digital solution that can undoubtedly aid in tracking individuals' health insurance status, even when they move from region to region, is online eligibility or insurance status checks. An online eligibility check is essentially about providing a digital option to check in real-time the eligibility or insurance status of an individual. This check shows whether an individual is suitable for admission to a health insurance scheme. It can also show in real-time whether an individual is currently insured in the scheme. The latter is often relevant for health service providers in countries where multiple health insurance schemes exist in parallel, such as in India.

BOX 10

Portability of Services in the EU

An excellent example of this is seen with the European Union (EU). Within the EU, the unrestricted mobility of workers between member states is one of the fundamental principles. To ensure this principle was adopted, the modernized social security coordination rules were developed, and specifically for health, they state that the utilization of health services falls under the jurisdiction of the state people live. If individuals stay temporarily in a different state, they are entitled to all benefits in kind, which they may require during their stay abroad, given that they are insured under a statutory health insurance scheme in their home country. To simplify the provision of medical care received while abroad, the European Health Insurance Card (EHIC) was created and is carried by each insured European citizen to facilitate this.

Source: Vollaard H. 2006. European Integration and Unfreezing Territoriality: The Case of the European Health Card. In: Holzhacker, R. and Haverland M., eds. *European Research Reloaded: Cooperation and Europeanized States Integration among Europeanized States.* Springer, Dordrecht.

---

13   Brickenstein, C. 2015. Social Protection of Foreign Seasonal Workers: From State to Best Practice. *Comparative Migration Studies.* 3 (2).

Online Eligibility Check-in Cambodia

In Cambodia, the National Social Security Fund (NSSF), which oversees the mandatory Social Health Insurance for private sector workers, developed an app that serves both NSSF members and the health service providers.

The app allows NSSF members to access their personal information and to monitor their works history and transaction statements. It makes contacting the NSSF more accessible.

Beneficiaries log in with an easy NSSF ID and can then proceed with functionalities such as finding a health facility or NSSF office close by, updating personal information, and viewing NSSF news.

The second group of functions of the app is targeted at health facilities and NSSF branches, constituting the eligibility check part. Indeed, it allows staff to search and check eligible beneficiaries when individuals approach health facilities seeking treatment. From a technical perspective, a role-based approach was taken. Only registered staff at a health facility are allowed to use (with login details) the app.

Screenshots of both the function for members and health facilities can be found in the annexures. The application has been introduced relatively recently and is experiencing some challenges, such as the app's speed, which software developers are working on to improve.

Source: National Social Security Fund. 2014. *Health Insurance Scheme*. [online] NSSF. Available from: http://www.nssf.gov.kh/default/health-care-scheme-2/ (accessed 2 February).

Employee Registration Platform in Germany

In Germany for instance, only certain programs that meet all requirements for data protection and transmissions security are permitted for electronic data transmission between employers and the Statuary Health Insurance Funds. One possibility is the electronic submission via the website sv.net. This enables employers to submit social health insurance notifications, contribution statements, reimbursement requests, and other certificates and messages to the social insurance agencies. Notifications and contribution statements are often generated by payroll accounting programs and are also transmitted to health insurers automatically. However, a prerequisite for participation in the automatic transmission, by the provisions of the Administrative Simplification Act, is that the payroll programs have passed a system test. The test is particularly required if an employer wants to submit the data with a noncertified software product (which is rarely the case).

Source: ITSG. 2021. *sv.net – Sozialversicherung im Internet*. [online] ITSG. Available from: https://www.itsg.de/produkte/sv-net/ (accessed 28 May).

Employee registration platforms

Employee registration platforms are all-digital solutions for the registration of workers and employees in statuary health insurance. Especially for the formal sector, it is often a great relief for larger companies if there is a standard electronic procedure for transferring information from the health insurance directly to employees.

In several contexts, the employers have their internal processes and IT systems to maintain their list of employees as well their payroll data. The linkage of these systems to health insurance information systems becomes important when it comes to managing the health insurance benefits provided to the same employees, especially when the risk carrier (or insurer who might or might not be an external entity) requires specialized software for management of health insurance benefits. There is hence a need for a regularly updated list of employees to be shared with the health insurance information system for the latter to establish the period in which the individual remains insured as well data related to pay grades, etc., that help establish the insurance contribution for the covered individuals as per defined structure. After this in certain contexts, employees could be provided access to the health insurance system to interact with their health insurance to track and be aware of their benefits, etc.

BOX 13

Employee Registration Platform in Nepal

Taking an example from the region, the Social Security Board or SSB (managing the scheme for the formal sector) has recently decided to apply the information system used by the Health Insurance Board or HIB (managing the scheme for the informal sector) for their insurance operations. HIB uses smartphone technology for its registration platform where, during the enrollment process, households are actively approached through door-to-door recruitment. Beneficiaries are enrolled with a form and a capture of their portrait picture with a smartphone. Forms and membership identity cards with QR codes are preprinted and given to the enrollment assistants before the process.

The SSB is now modifying the same software to facilitate the task of companies to be able to validate their employees through an online enrollment portal provided by openIMIS (that administers the claims for all employees). SSB continues to use its internal MIS (SOSYS) to manage employee lists and payroll information as well management of nonhealth benefits and uses openIMIS for management of the health insurance they provide. The list of employees is regularly updated by the employer in openIMIS (to manage the health insurance benefits) through direct access to an online portal. In case of a new employee, If the individual does not have a past health insurance ID (i.e., not existing already in openIMIS), the employer asks the person to be enrolled through an enrollment officer first in openIMIS. Then with the issued insurance ID, the employer can add the individual as their employee through their portal access and subsequently manage the individual in the same way as the other employees.

The calculation of due payments as per payroll information of respective employees is as well configured in openIMIS and forms part of the regular maintenance process from the side of the employer with regular checks by the insurance scheme. Based on updated employee lists, openIMIS generates regular invoices to the employer who then makes the payments and thereafter information is shared with openIMIS which accordingly updates the policy status. All subsequent transactions between health facility and insurer are thereafter managed in openIMIS, where facility staff can use mobile phone apps to verify the individual insurance status and eligibility as well as submit claims. A full workflow diagram can be seen on the source link provided.

Source: Rabovskaja, V. 2021. *Incubator: Support for Formal Sector Schemes*. [online] OpenIMIS Atlassian. Available from: https://openimis.atlassian.net/wiki/spaces/OP/pages/819003487/Incubator+Support+for+formal+sector+schemes (accessed 28 May).

BOX 14

Takeaways for Beneficiary Management

- Interoperability in the health sector, including government-supported health insurers, is hardly feasible without a unique identifier.
- Unique identifiers are as well important in countries having multiple insurance pools (typically formal and informal sector specific schemes) and increasingly looking at merging these.
- Beyond a unique identifier/number, a critical aspect is the authentication of a person, which is error and/ or fraud prone, and can be reduced by solutions applying biometric means (though trade-off with cost implication should to be evaluated).
- The choice for the correct ID number, which is supposed to increase interoperability, is not a technical but a political and strategic issue that plays an essential role.
- Mobile enrollment apps can be a great time saver for insurers and beneficiaries alike.
- An extension of enrollment apps into beneficiary self-management portals is a good idea, as the provision of real-time data exchange between patients, insurers, and health-care providers increases transparency and trust. The more solutions to reach the client and simplify the process the better, though target population profile/uptake of solution against cost is an important to-do.
- A prerequisite for using mobile enrollment solutions or self-management portals is an integrated Know-Your-Customer (KYC) function that serves to identify and authenticate a person uniquely.
- One way to improve the portability of health insurance benefits would be to improve the pooling function. To do this, making information management systems interoperable can help.
- The possibility of real-time eligibility checks for the insured person requires the integration of identity and authentication features. Data security must have the highest priority here.
- Data privacy needs according to respective country regulations have to be taken into consideration while designing apps and portals and enabling/improving data exchange.

Source: Authors.

Premium Management

Premium management involves tracking collected funds against respective individuals or households who are insured under the scheme. The payment of premium can be made in various ways, such as single or installment payments. Even third-party payments may be made where someone, or an institution, pays on behalf of the individual.

Having multiple transactions for a single policyholder can make it more complicated to track the payment. In addition, the calculation of payments varies depending on set prices for a specific insurance product or, as in many formal sector insurance programs, based on the pay grade of a person or overall income. These options hence lead to complicated requirements from the software solution needed to support premium management calculation and tracking in a health insurance system.

While payment frequency in principle is regularized due to the nature of insurance policy being prepaid and limited in validity/duration (leading to subsequent renewals of an existing policy at regular intervals, say a year), voluntary health insurance schemes especially targeting the informal sector try to offer more flexibility and possible means of collection money to increase their outreach and uptake. This goes beyond splitting the premium to smaller installments or alignment of payment frequency to the income cycle (where possible) of clients to attempting to influence client behavior by simplifying and/or providing more convenience to clients by expanding the modes of payment collection. With innovations in financial technologies, several solutions are as well linking to health insurance operators' digital solutions in this regard.

Additionally, health insurance systems generally work with separate accounting systems for payment methods such as cash, mobile money, or bank transfer—which could lead to complications for premium management, especially the tracking of payments.

NHI operators hence based on their needs, target audience, and available solutions need to have digital solutions that allow strong tracking of due premium versus actual payment status within the NHI digital system, as well flexibility in terms of the payment modes and sources of premium collection that they undertake.

Table 2: Key Drivers for Premium Management

Challenge/Key driver	Digital support opportunities
Flexibility in premium calculation methods	Module to manage contribution calculation
Transparency in incoming and outgoing payments	Payment tracking
Low transaction costs for individual contribution payers	Using mobile payment mechanisms Online eligibility check
Easier customer acquisition	Multiple payment options to give clients more options and make payments easier
Customers today want flexible payment methods throughout the year	Solutions allowing the collection of "annual contributions," depending on the ability to pay (seasonal) or in multiple payments where possible and applicable
Mobile wallets are already popular in many countries and so are cash-to-mobile solutions but might not be used to the full extent by health insurance operators	Mobile wallets Cash-to-wallet

Source: Authors.

Addressing the Key Drivers and Solutions from Other Countries

Payment tracking

Payment tracking, as mentioned previously, requires flexibility in terms of single or multiple payments, and accordingly activation of insurance policy, especially for informal sector schemes that offer insurance on a voluntary nature. Box 15 covers an informal sector scheme, whereas Box 16 shows how payment tracking solutions can be applied to a formal sector scheme.

BOX 15

Payment Tracking in Tanzania and Nepal for an Informal Sector Scheme

An example of how information systems track payments against a family's insurance policy is shown below, applied in Tanzania and Nepal (openIMIS). Single or multiple payments can be tracked against a policy that a family is enrolled under. The payment collected can come in different forms (mobile payment, electronic bank transfer, or in cash), made by the family itself or on behalf of the family by an external payer (partly or fully). The policies can be overridden and activated even with part payment if the scheme rules require this and otherwise all policies get automatically activated once payments are complete.

Source: OpenIMIS. 2021. *Nepal.* [online] Schweizerische Eidgenossenschaft, Federal Ministry for Economic Cooperation and Development, Deutsche Gesellschaft für Internationale Zusammenarbeit. Available from: http://openimis.org/nepal (accessed 2 February).

BOX 16

Payments in Kenya for a Formal Sector Scheme

The NHIF uses multiple web-based and mobile solutions to provide improved services and keep its members engaged.

The so-called "Payroll Byproduct" is used for the formal sector, which allows employers to pay the contributions for their employees.

The Payroll Byproduct was introduced to increase the efficiency and speed of collecting employers' monthly payroll by-products to the NHIF via the online Byproduct system. Instead of sending hard copy documents or e-mails to the NHIF, companies can just register and upload necessary data in a .xls and .xlsx format once they log in to the system.

Source: NHIF. 2021. *NHIF Service Charter.* [online] NHIF Kenya. Available from: http://www.nhif.or.ke/healthinsurance/serviceCharter (accessed 2 February).

Online and mobile solution-based contribution and/or premium payments

Beyond the collection of cash for premium payment, digital solutions have opened up the door to multiple modes of premium collection possibilities for health insurers. Here with online contribution payments, we refer to the payments of premium to the health insurer using different digital technology, some of which as well are mobile-based solutions. These can be done directly by a member of the scheme or by an employer, in single as well multiple and cumulative payments. We try to provide in this section a few examples of such solutions that health insurers have applied in different contexts to address distinct needs in given conditions.

While payments are made through electronic means (bank transfers, credit card payment, etc.), a lot of innovations have also been about mobile-based solutions to collect payments. Mobile money is one such solution (e.g.,

M-PESA) which is an alternate virtual banking system (mobile money service) that offers transaction services through a SIM card on a mobile phone.

The SIM card allows users to receive and store money, as well as make payments and transfer money to vendors and family members using SMS messages based on USSD interfaces (without the need for internet using even basic phones). These solutions had come into the market especially to address the problem that individuals in remote, underserved areas have limited access to formal banking systems and hence no bank accounts. The account here is managed by the telecom operator using the phone number as the defacto account number of an individual.

These mobile money transactions can also be used to transfer money into mobile money wallets where money can be collected to pay for specific expenses, e.g., health-care expenses, including health insurance premium payments.

BOX 17

Mobile Money Payments in Kenya

In Kenya, mobile payments are used to pay insurance premiums for the Kenyan public insurer. The National Hospital Insurance Fund (NHIF) provides accessible and affordable health insurance to Kenyans over the age of 18 with a monthly income of KES 1,000 and above. The NHIF registers all eligible members from both the formal and informal sectors, with compulsory membership for participants in the formal sector. The NHIF uses multiple web-based and mobile solutions to provide improved services and keep its members engaged.

To use these services, the user needs to register and consequently get an NHIF member number by SMS. This allows them to access self-care services, including monthly contributions, payment of penalties and arrears, and select a primary hospital of choice. The image shows the relatively straightforward procedure of paying contributions via M-Pesa.

In Kenya, the approach is that mobile payment solutions like MPESA are tied to specific telecom operators which provide these solutions and have their transactional charges. There are other competitive alternatives like T-Kash or Airtel Money.

Source: NHIF. 2021. *NHIF Service Charter.* [online] NHIF Kenya. Available from: http://www.nhif.or.ke/healthinsurance/serviceCharter (accessed 2 February).

In addition, several digital wallet solutions (including mobile app-based wallets) have come up in various country contexts where the digital wallet is linked to a bank account or credit and/or debit card. These wallets hence build on existing formal financial systems where money is transacted electronically through various solutions. There are multiple terms for digital or electronic wallets, but most refer to cashless payments on the internet. In simple terms, the user defines an amount with which he/she loads their virtual or digital wallet to be able to pay for various services electronically.

The mobile wallet can as well be an app that can be installed on a smartphone, or it is an existing built-in feature of a smartphone. A mobile wallet stores credit cards, debit cards, coupons, or reward cards information.[14] Once the app is installed and the user inputs payment information (bank account and/or e-banking account, credit card, etc.), the wallet stores this information by linking a personal identification format such as a number or key, QR code, or an image of the owner to each card that is stored.

These kinds of digital wallet products have become increasingly popular, given that digital transfers are becoming standard in most sectors. This is highlighted in the results of the GSMA's "State of the Industry Report" in 2019[15] that predicts the wallet market to grow rapidly.

BOX 18

Digital Wallets in India

A major player in the digital wallet sector is Paytm, based in India. This Indian e-commerce payment system and financial technology has become increasingly popular since its establishment in 2010 and is now considered a key feature of the Indian financial system. The Paytm Wallet was originally used as payment options for the Indian Railway, Uber, and other taxi services. It has then progressively expanded its reach to the payment of education fees, metro recharges, electricity, gas, and water bills, as well as insurance premiums.

Indeed, Paytm offers the possibility to pay insurance premiums directly through their portal. They have partnered with a list of health and life insurance companies such as Aditya Birla Health Insurance, Aviva Life Insurance, Max Bupa Health Insurance, and TATA AIA Life Insurance so their customers can pay their contributions through Paytm. The beneficiary simply needs to log in to Paytm.com, select the insurer, and enter the policy number and date of birth. Additionally, the user will benefit from several deals and offers when paying with Paytm.

This can significantly reduce transaction costs and administrative costs for agencies and individuals. A household can pay all bills and costs in one place and does not need to visit banks or insurance branches.

It is important to note here that the list of health insurers that offer this service through Paytm are all private companies. There would be an opportunity here for government insurers to take advantage of this offer and possibly envisage a public–private partnership where beneficiaries from the various government health schemes could pay their contributions through Paytm.

Source: Paytm. 2021. *Pay Your Insurance Premium*. [online] Paytm. Available from: https://paytm.com/insurance-premium-payment (accessed 27 May).

Considering the range of payment options, there have been technological innovations around various forms of aggregators (example in Box 19) which help health insurers bring together and manage the complexities of these payment methods and offer clients simpler and flexible solutions to pay.

---

14   Kenton, W. 2020. *Mobile Wallets*. [online] Investopedia. Available from: https://www.investopedia.com/terms/m/mobile-wallet.asp (accessed 2 February).
15   Naghavi, N. 2019. *State of the Industry Report on Mobile Money*. GSMA.

BOX 19

Mobile Money Payments (Aggregator) in Tanzania

Another interesting approach is applied by the Tanzanian government, which has simplified and unified government transactions through a Government Electronic Payment Gateway (GePG). Apart from a change in regulations that allow government transactions to be accepted through electronic forms including mobile money, a government-created semiautonomous agency (E-Government Agency or EGA) has designed GePG which is linked to banks and mobile money providers to facilitate electronic payment tracking for all government systems. The GePG has negotiated transaction rates and technologically connected all mobile phone operators to their solution, allowing clients in the country flexibility to use any mobile money provider to make payments to government programs including their public health insurance scheme. Clients wanting to make mobile money or bank transfers toward insurance payments can make a request through the USSD interface to the insurance system which then gets from the GePG system a control number that authorizes and helps track the payments through the GePG system and the insurance system.

This meant that technologies used by government programs such as the health insurance solution (iCHF-IMIS/openIMIS) applied by the public insurance scheme (improved Community Health Funds or iCHF that targets the informal sector) only needed to connect to GePG and did not need to build technological bridges with each mobile money provider. While programs initially had to link to mobile money solutions tied to specific telecom providers, this solution provided clients with more flexibility to make payments from any provider of their choice. At the same time, the solution for the insurance program provided an easy starting point to enable the collection of money in various forms (mobile money and bank transfers), already negotiated transaction rates (scale of transactions beyond transactions needed by health insurance program) as well existing tried and tested technological bridges to all mobile money providers in the country, which ultimately fit the iCHF plans to increase accountability and transparency in their health insurance system.

Source: Daily News Reporter. 2020. *Ministry Launches E-Payment Gateway Mobile App.* [online] Daily News. Available from: https://www.dailynews.co.tz/news/2020-01-145e1d7e69e5c30.aspx (accessed 27 May).

BOX 20

Takeaways for Premium Management

- With a fully automated, digitally supported premium collection system, the processing costs for the health insurance provider are lowered (compared to tracking needs in systems dependent on cash).
- Insurers should aim to offer alternate forms of payments acceptable in a given context and piggy back on existing innovations as well other value-added offers these solutions bring that can encourage insurance uptake.
- When offering alternative payment options, aggregators allowing management of multiple forms of payments are attractive solutions especially if they can reduce vendor (e.g., specific mobile money provider or a bank) dependence.
- The benefits of such a payment portal can go beyond the health sector and can lead to a much stronger social protection environment.

Source: Authors.

Provider Management

Provider management refers to all health insurance processes related to managing the medical professionals (such as a physician, nurse, dentist, therapist) or facilities (hospital, clinic, home health agency) that can claim payments under the insurance scheme. This management also includes registering a new provider under the scheme and establishing a contract with the health insurance, negotiating rates, and setting up a fee schedule.[16]

Although contract management between the insurer and the health-care provider can also get digital support by applying standardized document management software, it is not the focus of this chapter. A key aspect is instead the accessibility of the beneficiaries to the contract hospital or contract physician.

Within the framework of contract management, the performance expected from a service provider is often defined in contracts between the health insurer and the health service provider. Some KPIs within these contracts can focus on the way medical services are provided. This is not about choosing the right treatment method—but about service to the customer. Examples are the definition of maximum waiting times for patients, maximum periods in which claims can be submitted, but also attendance times of medical staff.

Table 3: Key Drivers for Provider Management

Challenge/Key driver	Digital support opportunities
Health insurers always want beneficiaries to use the health service providers with whom they have a contract	Provider locator apps Online eligibility check
Waiting times for the insured should be as short as possible. COVID-19 requires additional measures to prevent virus transmission	Online doctor appointments
Insurers want to intervene as early as possible when medical services were not provided, unjustified additional costs were charged, or no service orientation was apparent	Complaint management systems

Source: Authors.

Addressing the Key Drivers and Solutions from Other Countries

Provider locator apps
Health service provider locator apps refer to mobile services (e.g., smartphone apps) that allow the customer to find a doctor in their insurance network directly from their mobile device. They can also have additional functions such as patient reviews or direct booking of doctor's appointments. A popular platform in the United States is Zocdoc.[17]

Unfortunately, the available literature did not provide any comparable examples for provider locator apps of LMICs in the public sector.

---

[16]   Note: In Cambodia, the National Social Health Insurance Fund also contracts private facilities with different tariffs than public facilities. It is also possible that a primary facility pays a different rate for the same service than a tertiary facility.

[17]   Zocdoc. 2021. *About Us.* [online] Zocdoc. Available from: https://www.zocdoc.com/about/ (accessed 2 February).

Online doctor appointments

Technology that allows the booking of doctor's appointments online has been around for many years and has been implemented through various software worldwide. In the age of smartphones, the principle is the same, and app providers try to come up with more user-friendly and appealing interfaces.

The patient can book an appointment with a doctor, preferably one within the associated insurance network, directly and receive a booking confirmation. This confirmation gives individuals the flexibility to search for available appointments while allowing the health provider to manage patients flows better and reduce their administrative burden.

The authors deliberately avoided looking at individual doctor appointment apps in detail, as there is a flood of apps that all perform similar functions. The main difference between the apps is how they are integrated into the patient-provider-insurer triangle.

For example, the insurer can provide an app and is then only used to make appointments for these beneficiaries. From a technical perspective, the app must then be connected to the insurer's member database to carry out an eligibility check when making appointments via the app. Other models foresee that the patient only specifies his insurance company when making the appointment, but the app has no link to the respective insurer.

However, the seamless integration of such solutions is not easy to implement, as the corresponding health service provider must also administer the appointments that have been booked online. If the corresponding administrative capacities are not available and patients who have registered via the app cannot receive timely treatment, the added value of the digital solution is lost.

Complaint management systems

This report has intentionally refrained from covering examples of available software for complaint management systems as the international and in-country markets certainly provide a large number of implementable solutions off-the-shelf that can easily be adapted for health insurance operators.

Provider payment management

For provider payment management, the use of openIMIS in Tanzania and Nepal is given in Box 21.

BOX 21

Provider Contract Management in Tanzania and Nepal

An example of NHI solutions to manage provider payment arrangements is the openIMIS solution applied in Tanzania and Nepal. The solution allows the configuration of various price lists for different facilities, e.g., a standard price list for government health centers while different price lists for different private clinics, depending on what is negotiated.

Fixing price lists relate to a fee-for-service nature of provider contracts that are applied in Nepal through price revisions are as well made and the solution accordingly deals with the claims based on when the adjustments are made. In Tanzania as well provider payment mechanisms have changed over time. In the initial pilot phase

continued on next page

Box 21 continued

of the insurance scheme (CHF), hospitals were paid on a fee-for-service basis while primary care facilities (dispensaries and health centers) were paid on a relative pricing approach. The relative pricing approach placed a cap on the total amount to be paid out for a given period (a percentage of the total income of iCHF in that period), which was then distributed across the primary care facilities based on the number of insured clients treated by them. Hence, the facility treating more insured patients gets a higher share of the allocated amount. This translated to a payment per claim that was relative in each period as collection amount and patients treated varied in each time frame.

Subsequently, the current national approach applies the relative pricing concept for payment to hospitals while primary care facilities are now paid based on a capitation formula that again takes a share of the total amount collected by the scheme in a given period and distributes it based on the calculation of weights given to catchment population of a health facility, insured clients in the catchment area of that facility and number of insured clients treated at the facility. The solution hence allows more flexibility in remuneration arrangements for health facilities as well calculation of complex formulas (with the ability to configure weights and percentage share of allocations) to enable timely payments as per a scheme's rationale and provider payment approaches.

Source: OpenIMIS/2021. *Nepal.* [online] Schweizerische Eidgenossenschaft, Federal Ministry for Economic Cooperation and Development, Deutsche Gesellschaft für Internationale. Zusammenarbeit. Available from: http://openimis.org/nepal (accessed 2 February).

BOX 22

Takeaways for Provider Management

- Clients should quickly find the nearest contracted hospital or health facility. If GPS mapping has been done, mobile apps can be developed relatively easily and provide significant added value for the customer. Patient flows as well can be controlled to some extent.
- Long waiting times at the hospital are one of the main reasons for customer dissatisfaction. Appointment scheduling apps can help here—but implementation requires clearly defined business processes at the service provider in order to be able to process agreed appointments.
- Provider payment mechanisms are becoming more complex. The trend is toward NHIs trying out and based on experience evolving their provider payment mechanisms. Digital solutions are therefore needed to support the health insurer in adapting and mapping different mechanisms for the respective service providers and offering smooth transitions.

Source: Authors.

Claims Management

Claims management includes various processes related to submission, verification, and reimbursement of claims to health-care facilities.

More specifically, these operations include the following:
- Client verification of insurance status and eligibility
- Submission of claims (by a facility or an individual) as per agreed rates
- Verification of claims
- Calculation of claims
- Final processing of claims to get the total payment note for facilities for a given period
- Payment of claims
- Claims review process
- Possibility for health facilities to track and monitor payment status of their claims

An important and overarching challenge to keep in mind when thinking of technology for claims management is upscaling. Indeed, when a health insurance scheme starts to expand, the volume of claims can rapidly increase, which may cause difficulties in managing them.

Suppose a health insurance operator provides only a limited-service package to its customers or targets a small proportion of the population or has a limited number of health service providers contracted. In that case, most operational processes can be done without defining all operational business processes in detail, and strong ICT support is not always needed. This changes when the operator wants to further develop the scheme either in terms of the target audience or benefits package or extends coverage by contracting many additional health service providers.

Extending an insurance program from the formal sector to the informal economy or self-employed, for example, poses several challenges as these groups are not homogeneous. In some cases, such as the Lao People's Democratic Republic or Cambodia, the different target groups have historically various benefit packages or even different provider payment models. Besides, the mandate of an existing health insurance provider can extend "politically" overnight even though there is no organizational readiness.

To cope with these challenges requires the collaboration of a variety of institutional players. In practical terms, this also means:
- looking at existing national and social sector policies that have a link to health insurance,
- aligning potential interventions with existing national strategic plans and frameworks,
- respecting existing laws (e.g., set up by the Ministry of Telecommunications), and
- adding to or developing a proper law, strategy, or guideline on data security and privacy.

These factors will then help with the implementation of various technologies for health insurers, especially ones that support the claims process, as these are often highlighted as key emerging technologies in the insurance industry. Indeed, there is a desire to receive claims submissions electronically and to use intelligent algorithms (using AI) to identify any incorrect claims settlements and simultaneously detect fraud and abuse. This ambition might be attained soon, and some countries have already invested in electronic solutions for claims submissions.

The Republic of Korea's National Health Insurance is a good regional example in Asia and the Pacific where digital claims management is reducing fraud and abuse.[18]

Despite the enormous potential, critics claim that there will still always be a need for manual human involvement on top of the IT system, given that individual decisions are sometimes necessary, especially in the area of health where choices are not always clear-cut.

Table 4: Key Drivers for Claims Management

Challenge/Key driver	Digital support opportunities
Fast and uncomplicated processing of claims	Coverage status check and claim submission by the beneficiary Standard claims submission software/app for health-care providers Direct connection of digital patient management systems (providers) to health insurance systems Online eligibility check
Automation of standard claim approvals and rejections (management of claims for a high number of cases)	AI-supported claim approval

Source: Authors.

Addressing the Key Drivers and Solutions from Other Countries

Coverage status check and claim submission by the beneficiary

The example covered here is of a digital solution for insurance status and claim submission by the beneficiary, which gives beneficiaries the option to access their insurance data online. This gives control over the insurance policy, allows a view of billed services, and, if necessary, submits own reimbursement applications online (or just have them checked).

An international example, implemented in Europe and Asia, is the Allianz MyHealth app,[19] which streamlines medical claims submissions. Members using the free app provide details about their claim, take a picture of their medical invoice, and submit it to the company. It is the latest example of a health insurer leveraging mobile technology to meet customers' demand for a simpler claims-submission process and quick access to services, especially during medical emergencies.

The example of Allianz MyHealth was chosen deliberately, even though Allianz is a private insurer. It is only interesting for government-supported health insurers where an individual submission of claims by the insured takes place. As a rule, this rarely happens when the service provider sends the billing data directly to the insured person or a billing office. However, such an app can still bring added value for the insured person by displaying the processing status or the payments made by the insurer.

---

[18]   Logyoung, K. et al. 2014. A Guide for the Utilisation of Health Insurance Review and Assessment Service National Patient Samples. *Epidemiology and Health*. 36.

[19]   Global Health Insider. 2021. *Allianz MyHealth App Overhauls Claim Submissions within a Year.* [online] Global Health Insider. Available from: http://www.globalhealthinsider.com/news/allianz-myhealth-app-overhauls-claim-submissions-within-a-year (accessed 2 February).

At this point, variants are also thinkable, in which the insured person has to confirm that a corresponding medical service has also been provided by the doctor.

Claims submission by the health-care providers

Fast reimbursement from the insurer to the service provider is influenced, among other things, by how quickly and correctly the service provider submits the claims data. As a rule, three scenarios are distinguished here:

1. The service provider has patient management and/or electronic health record (EHR) system from which he can generate the claim directly. This is then sent electronically directly to the insurer (e.g., Nepal).
2. The service provider first sends the claim data to a billing office, which then checks the data and forward it to the insurer (e.g., the Republic of Korea).
3. The insurer enters the claim data to relieve the medical staff (e.g., Cambodia).

Variant 1 can be considered the most advanced, but it is also the most difficult to implement at a national level.

A very interesting approach can be found in Viet Nam, where Vietnam Social Security (VSS) leaves the choice of software completely up to the service provider but strictly specifies the digital format for claim data delivery.[20] Service providers can then decide for themselves which tool they want to use. Claims that do not comply with the specified data standards will be rejected by VSS.

Another interesting tool is found in Ghana, the Claim-it software used for the National Health Insurance Scheme. This is elaborated in Box 23.

BOX 23

Claims Submission in Ghana

The National Health Insurance Authority of Ghana (NHIA) has launched an app known as "Claim-it" for its claims submission process for the National Health Insurance Scheme, a form of national health insurance established by the government of Ghana to provide equitable access and financial coverage for basic health-care services to its citizens.

The app serves as a platform that allows health-care service providers credentialed by the NHIA to generate and submit claims. It replaces the manual cumbersome paper-based process that has been the cause of undue delay and standoffs between the scheme and its service providers. It can either be installed and used on a single computer or implemented as a network application with multiple users and be integrated into any existing Hospital Health Management System (HMS). The product was first piloted at a selected number of Greater Accra and Easters Regions facilities before fully launching in 2016.

continued on next page

---

20   Le, Q. N. et al. 2020. The Evolution of Social Health Insurance in Vietnam and Its Role Towards Achieving Universal Health Coverage. *Health Policy Open.* 1.

Box 23 continued

The developers and government officials who have been working on implementing the app have stated that the software has contributed to solving multiple problems, including the incident of fraud frequently within the National Health Insurance system. Furthermore, according to a report by PharmAccess, it has reduced the number of rejections that come in, which means it ensures providers submit the right type of claim. It also has the particularly advantageous feature of an offline mode, especially given the rural environment in which it applied, so users can work independently without the internet, only needing to connect for system updates and the actual submission of claims.

Source: NHIS. 2021. *NHIS Claim-it*. [online] National Health Insurance Scheme Ghana. Available from: http://claimit. nhia.gov.gh/ (accessed 2 February).

BOX 24

Takeaways for Claims Management

- Digitally supported claims management can bring significant time and cost savings for the insurer, but also for the service provider and ultimately for the insured.
- The efficient management of claims becomes especially critical in an upscaling process in which schemes are extended to the national level or the target group of insured persons is expanded, and the number of claims significantly increase.
- Fraud & abuse can be reduced by actively involving the insured person in the process of digital claim approval.
- The precise definition of data exchange standards by a national regulatory authority is very helpful for fast claim processing.
- Granular data captured in each claim (mix of patient treatment record and billing related information) is quite valuable for claims processing and beyond.
- Artificial intelligence opens up new ways for more efficient claims management, but requires good enough data to be able to "train" the digital algorithm.

Source: Authors.

A country example from the People's Republic of China (PRC) shows that claims management can be optimized through digitalization. For example, digitized claims processing at the point of service provision with real-time online copayment elements can eliminate the lengthy reimbursement processes. This lowers the financial burden on patients and purchasers.

Advanced Management Functions

Care management generally refers to a comprehensive span of services that assist patients with chronic or complex medical conditions and help them manage their health. This is becoming increasingly relevant for health insurance schemes in LMICS, where the disease burden from noncommunicable diseases (NCDs) is rising.[21]

Not only is chronic care important, but preventive care is also essential at helping reduce unnecessary treatments and helping people manage their health. Shifting the focus from hospital spending to more significant investment in health promotion and prevention can help people stay healthy for as long as possible rather than entering the health system.

Digital solutions can ensure that care teams, even if they consist of people from different organizations who have never met face-to-face, coordinate on a patient's personal needs and health progress. These chronic disease management plans can be communicated to patients and their physicians, with feedback on a patient's progress being relayed to the appropriate members of the care team. When looking at chronic disease management in the long term, which involves multiple discipline approaches, even small incremental improvements in coordination can pay off in the long term for health insurance providers. The costs of intelligent, digitally supported chronic disease management are likely to be lower in the long term than the curative care costs that would otherwise be incurred.

Below, in Boxes 25-27, are three country examples, each showing examples of digital support chronic disease management.

BOX 25

Chronic Care Management in the Republic of Korea

The Republic of Korea is relatively advanced in the implantation of digital software for care management. An integral part of this is the NHIS health information website (which is also in form of an app), Health-iN, which provides general information on various diseases and appropriate health-care services to the public. Using data from medical examinations, the app provides subscribers with personalized health information.

Patients can use the website and app for various purposes such as registering for the Chronic Disease Management Pilot Program and manage their treatment. Individuals who have enrolled in the program are given a blood pressure monitor and glucose meter for self-monitoring to enter their results into the Health-iN mobile app and receive direct feedback from a doctor. In terms of data sharing, Health-iN links the NHIS national health information database with the Ministry of Food and Drug Safety, the Korean Metrological Administration, and the Ministry of Environment, to get information on food poisoning, environmental and climate risks. It also integrates private social media information (e.g., tweets and blogs) to follow trends for major diseases and provides warnings to the public. Through this service, the public can check regional risks of major diseases, step-by-step action plans during emergencies, regional weather information, air pollution levels, medical trends, and social media information. Ultimately, this data-sharing approach aims to make peoples' lives healthier and safer, reducing the need for medical treatment.

Source: Yi, J. Y. et al. 2018. Self-management of Chronic Conditions Using mHealth Interventions in Korea: A Systematic Review, *Healthcare Informatics Research*. 24 (3).

---

21   World Health Organization. 2021. *The Global Health Observatory, Total NCD Mortality*. [online] WHO. Available from: https://www.who.int/data/gho/data/themes/topics/indicator-groups/indicator-group-details/GHO/total-ncd-mortality/ (accessed 2 February).

BOX 26

Chronic Care Management in Indonesia

The Indonesian national health insurer (BPJS) has launched a program named Prolanis for members who suffer from chronic diseases such as hypertension and diabetes. It is an integrated system that links the patient, the health insurer, family doctors in government health clinics and primary health-care centers, pharmacies, laboratories, and hospitals. The identification of eligible patients is made through the P-care information system. Once registered, data are sent to BPJS, which includes the number of visits, the individual's phone number (for electronic reminders), number of referrals, and home visits.

Source: Khoe, L. C. 2020. The Implementation of Community-Based Diabetes and Hypertension Management Care Program in Indonesia. *PLoS One.* 15 (1).

BOX 27

Preventive Care and Health Promotion in Germany

A recent study by the strategy consultancy Deloitte, on behalf of the National Association of Statutory Health Insurance Funds (GKV Spitzenverband) in Germany, showed how Germany, like many European countries, is experimenting with health insurance models where a healthy lifestyle is rewarded by additional service offers or even discount campaigns from the health insurance company. These "healthy behaviors" can be recorded digitally with wearable devices, for example, but also include, for example, attending regular preventive health-care services. This creates attractive analysis and control options with potentially positive effects on the quality of care and expenditure on services, while increasing the satisfaction of the insured. This shows the necessity of technology and digital patient records or even a national patient record because only through this can the health insurer get a comprehensive picture of the insured person and assess the "healthy lifestyle."

Source: ERNI Swiss Software Engineering. 2021. *Health Insurance Providers: The Winders of Digitalization in the Health-Care System.* [online] ENRI. Available from: https://www.betterask.erni/news-room/health-insurance-providers-the-winners-of-digitization-in-the-health-care-system/ (accessed 2 February).

Utilization Management

Utilization management refers to activities that try to identify trends in utilizing care, such as over-, under-, or misuse of benefits, optimizing pharmacy use, and validating appropriate use of prescribed medicines.

When looking at utilization management and the usage of patient records, it is important to distinguish between electronic medical records (EMRs) and EHRs. EMRs are a digital version of the paper charts in the clinician's office. EHRs do all of this but go further as they focus on the holistic health status of the patient, including information beyond the standard clinical data collected by the provider and gives a broader view of a patient's care.[22] EHRs are designed to reach out beyond the health organization that originally collects and compiles the information and is based on sharing information with other health-care providers such as laboratories and specialists. This allows information from all the clinicians involved in a patient's care to be collected in one place.

Remote access to EHRs allows managing a patient's health information on the go with a mobile electronic device, which allows the patient to access medical data, such as consultation results and lab results, request for prescription renewals, communicate with physicians, schedule appointments, and more.

There is vast literature on the positive effect of such online record portals, especially concerning the reduction of resource demand. A study conducted in the UK on the use of patient record access in 2014 (Fitton, C. et al.) showed that if 30% of patients access their electronic general practice record online at least twice a year, approximately 11% of yearly appointments would be saved. In the US, another study (Zhou, Y. Y. et al) showed that record access linked with secured messaging led to a 25% reduction in visits to primary care and a 14% reduction in telephone calls.

In Taipei,China, the National Health Insurance has found a way of tackling this complex issue of record sharing through their "Pharma Cloud" system. See Box 28 for more information.

BOX 28

Utilization Management in Taipei,China

Here, we bring in an example from Taipei,China, and their Pharma Cloud system. In recent years, the National Health Insurance has faced some financial pressure, and the government has tried to tackle the issue of patient record sharing. Taipei,China has a dense network of providers, and if people do not regularly seek care at a fixed facility, medical records end up disorganized between different clinics, which can lead to double prescribing or a detrimental mixing of drugs. This led to the adoption of the patient-centered "NHI PharmaCloud System" in 2013. It allows doctors at contracted providers to search a patient's drug prescription records over the previous 3 months, which include the following:

- The sources of the prescriptions
- The diagnosis behind the prescription
- The pharmacological effect of the drugs
- The names of the drugs' ingredients
- The drugs names, specifications, and pharmaceutical NHI codes
- Drug usage and dosage instructions
- Patient treatment dates
- Chronic disease refill prescription drug claim dates
- Drug amounts
- Number of drug administration days
- Calculation of the number of days of medicine that should be left for each prescription

continued on next page

---

22   Garrett, P. and Seidman, J. 2011. *EMR vs EHR – What Is the Difference?* [online] The Office of the National Coordinator for Health Information Technology. Available from: https://www.healthit.gov/buzz-blog/electronic-health-and-medical-records/emr-vs-ehr-difference (accessed 2 February).

To access the records, medical professionals must use a dual-card verification (i.e., the medical personnel's card and the patient's NHI card) with an exclusive card reader (containing a verification chip). The technology has been a success with all hospitals in Taipei,China being connected to it as of July 2015. This has improved medication safety and quality and encouraged professionals to take more initiative to care for patients, enhancing doctor–patient relationships. It has also empowered the patient to be more aware of medication safety.

Source: National Health Insurance Administration. 2021. *Handbook of [Taipei,China] National Health Insurance.* [online] NHIA. Available from: https://www.nhi.gov.tw/english/Content_List.aspx?n=C88A633AED8B7086 (accessed 2 February).

National Health Insurance Administration. 2020. *NHI MediCloud System.* [online] NHIA. Available from: https://www.nhi.gov.tw/english/Content_List.aspx?n=02BA04454AED80E0&topn=BCB2B0D2433F6491 (accessed 2 February).

Audit and Fraud

Audit and fraud management is an important part of ensuring the efficiency and sustainability of a health insurance scheme or fund. This involves somehow identifying the fraudulent cases by identifying unusual patterns and then managing these cases appropriately. If this is done manually by medical reviews, this can be a very administratively burdensome process. Technology can certainly make it easier. Overarching digital IDs and national health information systems, for instance certainly allow for efficient tracking of fraudulent cases. This can be seen in Estonia. The use of AI for claims review is another way used in the Republic of Korea for example (Box 30).

These types of systems have not come without challenges. This is especially true for data privacy issues. In Asia and the Pacific, digitalization has made great progress in recent years; however, this does not mean that the target group for health insurance has digital literacy to use digital services or is aware of wider issues such as data privacy.[23] There is also the risk of data misuse by various stakeholders. It is therefore important to invest in measures for monitoring and clearly defined data privacy governance. Estonia, for example, is a small country and therefore was able to invest in digital literacy for the entire population over 2 decades. A comparison with Asian countries should be done carefully as the digital literacy rate differs widely (between countries but also between rural and remote areas).

A valuable lesson for governments in Asia and the Pacific is certainly the Estonian way of creating the "audit trail" as the solutions allow every citizen to see in real-time who is looking at their health data (Box 29).

---

[23]   ITU. 2021. *Digital Trends in Asia and the Pacific 2021: Information and Communication Technology Trends and Developments in the Asia-Pacific Region, 2017-2020.* ITU Publications.

BOX 29

Digital Audit in Estonia

There are 1.3 million citizens in Estonia, and every citizen and every resident has a unique ID number, and the country is very advanced in terms of digitalization. In Estonia, 88% of households have a broadband connection (2015), 82% of households use a mobile Internet connection (2016), 96% of income tax declarations are made via the e-tax board (2016), 32% of votes were cast over the internet (2017), and 99% of bank transfers are carried out electronically. In 2001, the digital invoicing system for electronic transfer of reimbursement claims, called Estonian Health Insurance Fund (EHIF), was launched.

In 2002, the law obliged all pharmacies to transmit the prescription information for reimbursement to the EHIF electronically. Over 75% of health-care providers and 45% of all pharmacies had signed data transmission contracts. In 2005, all the reimbursement claims and prescription data in Estonia were submitted electronically. Furthermore, the country has implemented a so-called Estonian nationwide Health Information System (EHIS). EHIS also hosts many central registers and databases such as hospitals, family doctors (general practitioners), pharmacies, school nurses, medicine interactions, and different quality registers (cancer, HIV, tuberculosis, etc.). Furthermore, it utilizes several nationwide registers such as the population and the business register. One of the crucial parts of EHIS is the patient portal. Using the patient portal, the user can:
- log in with an ID card or mobile ID,
- view and update personal data and add contact data of close relatives,
- view his/her medical data from health-care providers,
- view electronic referral letters and electronic prescriptions,
- add representatives for him/herself for actions such as collecting e-prescriptions,
- make declarations of intent (e.g. donation of organs),
- access health insurance data,
- hide sensitive health data from doctors and representatives,
- complete a health declaration form before an appointment, and
- view the log of who has accessed his and/or her data (audit trail).

The key feature here is that if a nurse or doctor opened the Electronic Medical Record of a specific person, he and/or she would need to sign in with a Doc/Nurse ID number to pull the record. A citizen who logs into his and/or her "my health" portal could automatically see which doctor/nurse has retrieved which information from the medical record. This principle does not only apply to the health sector but all e-government services. A citizen would see if a police officer looks onto a particular dataset (exact timestamp is given) without permission to do that.

Source: Metsallik, J. et al. 2019. *Ten Years of the e-Health System in Estonia.* Department of Health Technologies, Tallinn University of Technology.

BOX 30

AI Use in the Republic of Korea

The Republic of Korea is a good example of how the use of artificial intelligence (AI) can help in the reduction of incorrect and fraudulent claims. The Government of the Republic of Korea's initial focus has been on improving medical care through AI algorithms and is already in use for automatic claims processing within the Health Insurance Review and Assessment Service (HIRA), their semiautonomous claims review institution.

Smart audit algorithms enable reliable identification of those, and only those, claims that are incorrect. A multistage system usually does this. In a first step, all applications received are examined to check whether correct and unusual claims are filtered out. Artificial intelligence is then used to identify correlations between unusual claims, which help determine the likelihood of successful intervention; the system learns with each new application.

An especially important finding for other countries is that the Republic of Korea started many years ago to set up the central Heath Insurance Database. The availability of "Big Data" allowed the development of intelligent algorithms and train the system successfully with sufficient data.

Source: Young-Hak, K. 2019. *South Korea Government Blueprint on Healthcare A.I. Asan Medical Centre, University of Ulsan College of Medicine.*

On the issue of AI development, it is important to note that AI is a specialization, which is difficult to learn. It requires lots of experience and a particular combination of skills to create algorithms that can teach machines to think, improve, and optimize business workflows.

Indeed, AI is very powerful; however, AI algorithms only work if the organization has a precise idea of what is to be achieved and if there is good existing data from which the algorithm can learn. Therefore, before starting, high-quality data must be available.

This means that in practice, the dataset needs to be:
- free from incoherent information,
- as accurate as possible, and
- with all the necessary attributes required for an algorithm to perform its task.

Even the most advanced algorithms in the world cannot deliver the desired results if there is no high-quality data to work with.

BOX 31

Takeaways for Advanced Management Functions

- Fraud and audit control is important for all health insurers.
- An essential point for successful fraud & abuse management is the availability of a lifelong identification number and authentication procedure for the beneficiary, ideally across all social protection branches and linked to biometric verification.
- Online platforms through which the insured can see the billed services of his service provider offer advantages. It enables immediate intervention if billed services are not provided, or the service quality is below the defined standards.
- As scheme size increases, artificial intelligence (AI) can help automate the claim approval process. Smart audit algorithms enable reliable identification of those claims that are incorrect. Good data quality is an essential prerequisite for the implementation of AI solutions.
- Data captured by insurers is a valuable source of information that can be used in various ways (cost control to improving chronic care management) at times going beyond the traditional role of collecting claims and making payments.
- Patient data management can take different forms (e.g., external patient portals instead of dedicated insurance systems) and impacts insurers, here data privacy needs of respective contexts need to be taken into account while designing solutions.

Source: Author.

Conclusions

This report focused on opportunities and good practices of integrating new technologies into government-supported health insurance schemes and highlighted successful examples of improvements in health insurance management and administration through digitization and innovative technologies.

Concrete examples, mainly in LMICs when possible, were used to show how digital solutions can successfully be implemented and used to improve NHI business processes. However, it was challenging to find these examples, as there is little publicly available documentation on products and digital interventions in use by government-supported health insurance operators. The lack of documentation was especially evident for developing countries. Therefore, some examples from developed countries or the private sector were presented.

A critical point that became clear during the analysis is that there is no "best" or "most appropriate" solution for a particular country when selecting digital products to support the health insurer. Country contexts vary widely, and so does the complexity of the public health financing and e-health landscape. Therefore, the potential transferability of a particular digital solution needs to be assessed on an individual basis.

Nevertheless, the authors have attempted to offer specific patterns that distinguish successful digital projects from the least successful ones. While the central part of this report provides a collection of available digital solutions, innovative ideas, and approaches, it also aims to facilitate decision-making on investments for potential digital interventions for government-supported health insurers by presenting several key messages for the implementation of digital solutions that have become apparent through this report.

Digital health strategies

First, the analysis indicated the enormous potential of digital products and the power of data. Economies such as the Republic of Korea and Taipei,China have an advanced, high level of digital maturity, and for about 10 years, have already invested in digital health strategies, which have evolved into a robust data-use culture among the actors in their health system. In addition, these economies have, among other things, created clear legal frameworks that regulate data exchange, data security, and data protection.

It is observed that countries with a clear vision, mission, and strategy for the long-term goals to be achieved in the health sector are also more successful in selecting appropriate digital products. Governments should understand that a digital tool or product should always generate significant added value, usually time or cost savings for users and stakeholders.

An existing digital health strategy, which provides a direction for the health sector for the upcoming years, makes it easier to assess the benefits of potential digital intervention and whether it would contribute to the overall mission of the NHI. If a potential digital solution does not contribute to the strategic goals, it may be a questionable investment.

Promoting in-country digital exchange hubs

Looking at different country contexts has shown that the fragmentation of existing digital solutions in health financing is exceptionally high in some countries. Historically, such fragmentation is often because individual institutions want to implement practical digital solutions more quickly for their specific target groups as part of their mandate.

The risk here is that politicians will sometimes promote a more charismatic technology that they perceive looks good rather than either practical or meeting the longer-term needs. Some countries have cleverly avoided these risks by creating an official digital exchange hub that is actively managed by a ministry rather than an individual minister.

A digital exchange hub provides a meeting space where government institutions, development partners, and private sector staff can convene and actively discuss and contribute to the government's digital plans. The aim is to avoid parallel and uncoordinated investments and to avoid adding more data silos that are increasing digital fragmentation.

Especially for health insurers, cross-sectoral exchange meetings with the stakeholders mentioned previously are of great help, and for whom digital interfaces to service providers, identification systems, CRVS systems, and payment providers can be essential.

Private health insurance

Although the primary focus of this report is not on private health insurance, it is worth noting that while public health insurers are most interested in using digital products, many technical innovations are coming from private health insurers. As private insurers, perhaps due to their for-profit nature, have a much greater interest in detailed datasets to assess insurance contracts for underwriting individuals, making predictions about potential health risks, improving efficiency and beyond (e.g., the trend of monetization of data), has lead to more innovative examples of digital solutions that are notable.

Especially in service optimization, government-driven health insurers can still learn a lot from private insurers. Particularly worthy of mention are innovations that promote a healthy lifestyle, digitally manage patient flows, shorten waiting times for claims processing, or reduce copayments.

Beneficiary management and identification systems

The first core businesses process covered in this report was beneficiary management. It became apparent through research that, in the past, the lack of proper coordination of health-care programs has often led to high transaction costs and inefficiencies for the insurer.

A substantial reason for these inefficiencies is that each stakeholder in the health system, including health insurers, maintains its member databases, but these databases are not interconnected. It is therefore difficult to track the patient across different health insurers or social protection providers. This is typically the case in some countries in Asia and the Pacific having a public insurance entity for the formal sector and a different one for the informal sector, where they use their respective information systems and ID numbers.

Effective digital beneficiary management can improve insurers' cost efficiency and customer satisfaction. Countries with a solid beneficiary management system have prioritized identification and authentication, often as part of a digital health strategy, and have also considered cross-sectoral investment opportunities.

Identification numbers are the "digital glue" that connects existing IT systems and underlying databases, reducing redundancy and complexity. The various digital solutions considered for this report indicated that unless a patient is first uniquely identified and authenticated, implementing digital products like customer-centric apps, e-health portals, m-health applications, and others would also likely not be successful.

Therefore, governments should work on a lifelong, unique identification number for the health sector on which all stakeholders in the health system and health insurers can rely and remain in existence for life. There are several ways to create a lifelong ID with appropriate authentication mechanisms. However, further elaboration would go beyond the scope of this report.

Outreach and premium management

Providing insurance to residents who do not have bank accounts has always been a challenge in developing countries, especially for voluntary health insurance schemes. Various examples from countries in Africa and in Asia and the Pacific show that mobile phone apps can solve several problems: Better outreach is possible, especially in rural areas, as Unstructured Supplementary Service Data (USSD)-based solutions, apps, or social media can communicate with existing or future policyholders.

Great value is added when premium payment is linked to digital payment options via mobile phones, avoiding the need for the beneficiary to travel to a payment point. The key here is collaborating with mobile payment service providers and telecommunication providers to keep transaction costs as low as possible.

Governments and development partners should take a cross-sectoral approach to promote alternate payment forms. Instead of signing individual contracts with different mobile payment providers and promoting multiple technical gateways, investments should be considered in cross-government payment platforms. A cross-government payment hub can create benefits that go far beyond the needs of health insurance.

Provider management

Health-care provider contracts can change in time, and especially provider payment mechanisms can become more complex. NHIs increasingly apply specific approaches and formulae, and based on experience, evolve their provider payment mechanisms. Digital solutions are therefore needed to support the health insurers in adapting and mapping different mechanisms for the respective service providers and offering smooth transitions.

Claims management

Digital support for more efficient claims management is very high on the wishlist of many national health insurers because this can bring significant time and cost savings for the insurer and the service provider and ultimately for the insured. In claims management, different variants of digital support exist where individual-level and good-quality data are very valuable for health insurers.

As pointed out throughout this report, some countries are more advanced than others in defining data standards and regulations for data exchange. The advantage of regulated data exchange becomes visible during claims management as well. Examples from the Republic of Korea and Viet Nam have shown how important it is for the service provider to deliver the claim data in a standardized format which was defined through clear government policies to support the administrative claims procedure.

Based on research for this regional report, but also on the personal experience of the authors, two scenarios for claim submissions were identified:
1. Either the health service providers can decide which software they want to use to submit the claim, but for the claim to be accepted, it needs to comply with specified data standards.
2. The government provides certified software solutions for which interfaces for claim submission are already available and ready to use by health service providers.

Audit and fraud

Audit and fraud management are assigned primarily to the area of claims management, as this is where the most significant risk of fraud or false billing lies. A valuable lesson for governments in Asia and the Pacific is undoubtedly the Estonian way of creating the "audit trail," as the solutions allow every citizen to see in real-time who is looking at their health data and what has been billed. The simple involvement of the insured person, who can mark incorrect information, already contributes significantly to error-free billing. While such approaches might be some steps away for certain countries, efforts around the automation of claims processing can still certainly add value.

A critical lesson regarding the use of AI for claims management is the need for high-quality data. Even the most advanced algorithms in the world will not work if the raw data quality is poor.

Care management and utilization management

Care management refers to a comprehensive range of services that support patients with chronic or complex conditions and help them manage their health. Care management is crucial for health insurers in LMICs, where the burden of disease from NCDs is increasing.

Health insurers in European countries have been promoting preventive health care for many years to keep people healthy for as long as possible, rather than paying high costs for curative care. Some insurance companies go one step further and reward a healthy lifestyle with monetary bonus points.

The analysis of the different countries in this report has shown that curative care management and case management also require good provider management. Chronic disease management costs are likely to be lower in the long run than the otherwise incurred curative care costs.

However, digital tools only help when all actors are willing to enter the relevant disease and treatment data into a centralized ICT system. In very advanced countries, national patient registries and personal health records are used, in which patient data are stored under strict data privacy conditions. These are made available to the health insurer. The insurers can then create digital solutions based on high-quality data.

Finally, governments should separate two high-level goals when considering digital interventions:
1. The collection of aggregated anonymized data at the national level to inform health financing mechanisms. These mechanisms include data extraction from operational systems (e.g., health insurance management system, patient management system) aggregated for analysis (e.g., DHIS2 system).
2. The collection of patient-specific data enables active case management and aims to actively manage patient flows and create a customer-centered experience.

In recent years, development partners have contributed enormously to M&E systems without creating an awareness that the raw data—coming from the operational systems—must be of appropriate quality. Health insurance data systems (especially around claims) include patient-level data that are highly valuable, which insurers can apply in different ways, as seen in this report.

A systemic transformation to a "data use" culture takes time but can be usefully supported by ADB.

Looking ahead, the authors hope that overall investments will be made to help governments define the digital business processes needed for health insurance and to help digitally integrate the health insurance system into the larger digital health space. In addition, supporting digital linkages between health-care providers and health insurance applications will be critical to building a coherent and interoperable digital health system. Finally, the government should work on customer-centric solutions and promote health-care interventions. Better digital linkages between health insurers, health service providers but also e-government initiatives will help to achieve the ultimate goal of increased access to affordable health services.

References

Asian Development Bank. 2018. *Guidance for Investing in Digital Health. ADB Sustainable Development Working Paper Series*. Manila.

Asian Development Bank. 2016. *Identity for Development in Asia and the Pacific*. Manila.

Brickenstein, C. 2015. Social Protection of Foreign Seasonal Workers: From State to Best Practice. Comparative Migration Studies. 3 (2).

Bui et al. 2021. Big Data for Public Health Surveillance in Vietnam: Challenges and Opportunities. In: Kreinovich V. and Hoang Phuong N., eds. *Soft Computing for Biomedical Applications and Related*. Springer International Publishing.

Capgemini. 2020. *Health Insurance Top Trends 2021*. Capgemini.

Daily News Reporter. 2020. *Ministry Launches E-Payment Gateway Mobile App*. [online] Daily News. Available from: https://www.dailynews.co.tz/news/2020-01-145e1d7e69e5c30.aspx (accessed 27 May).

Elbel, G. K. et al. 2019. *Digitalisierung des Gesundheitsmarktes*. Monitor Deloitte.

ERNI Swiss Software Engineering. 2021. *Health Insurance Providers: The Winders of Digitalization in the Health-Care System*. [online] ENRI. Available from: https://www.betterask.erni/news-room/health-insurance-providers-the-winners-of-digitization-in-the-health-care-system/ (accessed 2 February).

Fitton, C. et al. 2014. The Impact of Patient Record Access on Appointments and Telephone Calls in Two English General Practices: A Population-Based Study. *London Journal of Primary Care*. 6 (1). pp. 8-15.

Gelb, A. and Clark, J. 2013. *Identification for Development: The Biometrics Revolution*. Centre for Global Development.

Garrett, P. and Seidman, J. 2011. *EMR vs EHR – What Is the Difference?* [online] The Office of the National Coordinator for Health Information Technology. Available from: https://www.healthit.gov/buzz-blog/electronic-health-and-medical-records/emr-vs-ehr-difference (accessed 2 February 2021).

Global Health Insider. 2021. *Allianz MyHealth App Overhauls Claim Submissions within a Year*. [online] Global Health Insider. Available from: http://www.globalhealthinsider.com/news/allianz-myhealth-app-overhauls-claim-submissions-within-a-year (accessed 2 February 2021).

Handayani, P. W. 2018. Critical Success Factors for Mobile Health Implementation in Indonesia. *Heliyon*. 4 (11).

Hargrave, M. 2020. [online] Investopia. Available from: https://www.investopedia.com/terms/i/insurtech.asp (accessed 16 April).

Holz, J. 2021. *NCDs Threatening Health Insurance: Innovations, Partnerships Offer Ways to Mitigate the Impact*. [online] Next Billion. Available from: https://nextbillion.net/ncds-health-insurance/ (accessed 16 April 2021).

ITSG. 2021. *sv.net – Sozialversicherung im Internet*. [online] ITSG. Available from: https://www.itsg.de/produkte/sv-net/ (accessed 28 May 2021).

Joint Learning Network for Universal Health Coverage. 2018. *Using Health Data to Improve Universal Health Coverage: Three Case Studies*. PATH.

Joint Learning Network for Universal Health Coverage. 2019. *A Guide to Common Requirements for National Health Insurance Information Systems*. PATH.

ID4D. 2021. *ID4D Data: Global Identification Challenge by the Numbers*. [online] The World Bank Group. Available from: https://id4d.worldbank.org/global-dataset (accessed 16 April 2021).

Kang, M. et al. 2019. *Korean Resident Registration System for Universal Health Coverage*. World Bank Group.

Kenton, W. 2020. *Mobile Wallets*. [online] Investopedia. Available from: https://www.investopedia.com/terms/m/mobile-wallet.asp (accessed 2 February 2021).

Khoe, L. C. 2020. The Implementation of Community-Based Diabetes and Hypertension Management Care Program in Indonesia. *PLoS One.* 15 (1).

Labrique A. B. et al. 2018. Best Practices in Scaling Digital Health in Low and Middle-Income Countries. *Globalization and Health.* 14 (103).

Le, Q. N., et al. 2020. The Evolution of Social Health Insurance in Vietnam and Its Role Towards Achieving Universal Health Coverage. *Health Policy Open.* 1.

Logyoung, K. et al. *2014.* A Guide for the Utilisation of Health Insurance Review and Assessment Service National Patient Samples. *Epidemiology and Health.* 36.

Metsallik, J. et al. 2019. *en Years of the e-Health System in Estonia.* Department of Health Technologies, Tallinn University of Technology.

Mills, S. et al. 2019. Unique Health Identifiers for Universal Health Coverage. *Journal of Health, Population and Nutrition.* 38 (22).

Naghavi, N. 2019. *State of the Industry Report on Mobile Money.* GSMA.

Government of Taipei,China, Ministry of Health and Welfare, National Health Insurance Administration. *Health Insurance: Your Ticket to Well-Being (2020–2021).*

National Health Insurance Administration. 2020. *NHI MediCloud System.* [online] NHIA. Available from: https://www.nhi.gov.tw/english/Content_List.aspx?n=02BA04454AED80E0&topn=BCB2B0D2433F6491 (accessed 2 February 2021).

National Social Security Fund. 2014. *Health Insurance Scheme.* [online] NSSF. Available from: http://www.nssf.gov.kh/default/health-care-scheme-2/ (accessed 2 February 2021).

NHIF. 2021. *NHIF Service Charter.* [online] NHIF Kenya. Available from: http://www.nhif.or.ke/healthinsurance/serviceCharter (accessed 2 February 2021).

NHIS.2021. *NHIS Claim-it.* [online] National Health Insurance Scheme Ghana. Available from: http://claimit.nhia.gov.gh/ (accessed 2 February 2021).

Odeyemi, I. A. 2014. Community-Based Health Insurance Programmes and the National Health Insurance Scheme of Nigeria: Challenges to Uptake and Integration. *International Journal for Equity in Health.* 13 (20).

OpenIMIS. 2021. *Nepal.* [online] Schweizerische Eidgenossenschaft, Federal Ministry for Economic Cooperation and Development, Deutsche Gesellschaft für Internationale Zusammenarbeit. Available from: https://openimis.org/nepal (accessed 2 February 2021).

Satrina, S. 2020. *Easing Access to the National Health Insurance through a Mobile Application, Social Protection Floors in Action: 100 Success Stories to Achieve Universal Social Protection and SDG 1.3.* International Labour Office.

Stewart, M. 2019. *The Limitations of Machine Learning.* [online] Medium. Available from: https://towardsdatascience.com/the-limitations-of-machine-learning-a00e0c3040c6 (accessed 2 February 2021).

Paytm. 2021. *Pay Your Insurance Premium.* [online] Paytm. Available from: https://paytm.com/insurance-premium-payment (accessed 27 May).

PharmAccess Group. 2017. *NHIA of Ghana Launches Claims Payment Application.* [online] PharmAccess Group. Available from: https://www.pharmaccess.org/update/11388/ (accessed 2 February 2021).

Rabovskaja, V. 2021. *Incubator: Support for Formal Sector Schemes.* [online] OpenIMIS Atlassian. Available from: https://openimis.atlassian.net/wiki/spaces/OP/pages/819003487/Incubator+Support+for+formal+sector+schemes (accessed 28 May 2021).

Seong, S. C. 2015. *National Health Insurance System of Korea.* National Health Insurance Service.

United Nations. 2021. *Goal 3: Ensure Healthy Lives and Promote Well-Being for All at All Ages.* [online] United Nations. Available from: https://www.un.org/sustainabledevelopment/health/ (accessed 20 May 2021).

Vitality. 2021. *How We Work Out Your Health Insurance Renewal Premium.* [online] Vitality. Available from: https://www.vitality.co.uk/health-insurance/renewal-rates/ (accessed 16 April 2021).

Vollaard, H. 2006. European Integration and Unfreezing Territoriality: The Case of the European Health Card. In: Holzhacker, R. and Haverland M., eds. *European Research Reloaded: Cooperation and Europeanized States Integration among Europeanized States.* Springer, Dordrecht.

World Health Organization. 2020. *Global Strategy on Digital Health 2020-2025.* [online] WHO. Available from: https://www.who.int/docs/defaultsource/documents/gs4dhdaa2a9f352b0445bafbc79ca799dce4d.pdf (accessed 2 February 2021).

World Health Organization. 2021. *The Global Health Observatory, Total NCD Mortality.* [online] WHO. Available from: https://www.who.int/data/gho/data/themes/topics/indicator-groups/indicator-group-details/GHO/total-ncd-mortality/ (accessed 2 February).

Yi, J. Y. et al. 2018. Self-management of Chronic Conditions Using mHealth Interventions in Korea: A Systematic Review. *Healthcare Informatics Research.* 24 (3).

Young-Hak, K. 2019. *South Korea Government Blueprint on Healthcare A.I.* Asian Medical Centre, University of Ulsan College of Medicine.

Zendrive. 2021. *Company Meet.* [online] Zendrive. Available from: https://www.zendrive.com/company (accessed 20 May 2021).

Zocdoc. 2021. *About Us.* [online] Available from: https://www.zocdoc.com/about/ (accessed 2 February 2021).

Zhou, Y. Y. et al. 2007. Patient Access to an Electronic Health Record with Secure Messaging: Impact on Primary Care Utilization. *American Journal of Managed Care.* 12, pp. 418–424.